First Lady Blues

Toni Terry Savage

First Lady Blues

ISBN: 9798314708170

Dedication

This book is dedicated to my son, Terrell. He published his first writing in the 10th grade and is no longer here physically to cheer me on, but I feel his presence as I take on this new project of book writing. I have been journaling since the 6th grade and just found the motivation and time to write. I encourage others to tackle an idea or hobby that you've always thought about doing. This has been therapeutic for me. It might be for you too.

Secondly, I want to thank my cousins Katrina, Naderiah, and Nylah who were my rocks during my grieving and healing process.

Lastly, I also want to thank my mother for being a support, even when we disagree. Love ya sis.

Table of Contents

Introduction

"I hate my mother."

That was one of the earliest conversations Warren had with me back in 1995. Looking back now, that should have been a red flag, a bright neon sign warning me of all the unspoken pain and trauma hidden beneath his surface. But in the moment, I brushed it off, chalked it up to him being honest, maybe even vulnerable. I didn't realize those three words were a glimpse into a much deeper story—his story, my story, and eventually, *our* story.

This book is about the journey that began in that moment and how it spiraled into something far more complex and transformative than I ever imagined. It's about love and loss, faith and betrayal, strength and weakness, and ultimately, resilience. *First Lady Blues* isn't just my story; it's a story that has played out in countless lives, across time, in different ways. It's about the storms we face and the choices we make to either weather them or let them destroy us.

As you turn these pages, you'll walk with me through the pivotal moments of my life—the roots of my relationship with Warren, the childhoods that shaped us, and the magnetic pull that kept bringing us back to each other, even when life took us in opposite directions. You'll see how we reconnected during a global pandemic and stepped into what felt like a fairy tale, only to find ourselves standing on a foundation built on sand.

You'll feel the tension rise as financial struggles, broken trust, and unspoken wounds deepen the cracks in our marriage. And then you'll feel the full force of the storm—the tragedy that shook my family to its core and revealed truths that couldn't be ignored.

But this book isn't just about heartbreak. It's about the aftermath, the rebuilding, and the redemption. It's about how I found my way back to myself and learned to rise from the ashes of devastation. Along the way, I discovered truths about resilience, faith, and the power of transformation that I hope will inspire you to do the same.

The issues I share in these pages—generational trauma, grief, broken relationships, and the search for purpose—aren't unique to me. They've plagued people for generations. But here's the good news: you don't have to stay stuck in the pain. You don't have to let the storms of life define you.

As you journey through *First Lady Blues*, I invite you to reflect on your own life, your own challenges, and your own opportunities for growth. Let this book be more than a story; let it be a mirror, a guide, and a call to action.

Because if there's one thing I've learned, it's this: storms will come. But you have the power to rise, rebuild, and find beauty on the other side. The journey won't be easy, but I promise you—it will be worth it.

So, turn the page, and let's begin. Together, we'll uncover the lessons, the heartbreaks, and the triumphs that can transform not just my life but yours as well.

Welcome to *First Lady Blues*.

Chapter One

In the Beginning

(Genesis 1:1 - "In the beginning, God created the heavens and the earth.")

It was 1995. The year I met Warren at Jessup Pre-Release Unit. I was a correctional officer working hard to build the kind of life I could be proud of, and he was visiting a mutual friend, Byrd Sweeney. It wasn't the kind of place you'd expect sparks to fly, but from the moment our paths crossed, something about Warren captured my attention.

Warren had a presence that was hard to ignore. He was tall and slim and had on a light brown suit with a bow tie. He wasn't loud or flashy, but there was an undeniable confidence in the way he carried himself. His clean-cut appearance and the way he held his head high gave the impression that he had a plan, a vision even. He looked like someone who had been through a lot but was determined to come out on top. And I'll admit, that intrigued me.

At the time, my life was structured, almost to a fault. I was raising my two-year-old son on my own, even though I had a tremendous village, I was working long hours in a demanding job, and pushing through my bachelor's degree in criminal justice. Every day was a balancing act of responsibilities and ambitions. It wasn't glamorous, but it was steady. Predictable. Warren was none of those things, and that made him stand out.

He wasn't just another face passing through Jessup. There was something about him—something magnetic. He seemed like a man with ambition, someone who was going places, or at least trying to. Maybe it was the way he talked about starting his own upholstery business, a skill he'd picked up during his time in prison. Maybe it was the way he carried himself, like he was already living the life he wanted, even if the reality didn't quite match.

The First Impression

When I first saw Warren, I thought, *This man is going places.* I didn't see the reality of his circumstances—a man recently released from prison, unemployed, and living in public housing with his sister. I saw potential. I saw someone who, despite the weight of his past, had a certain charm that made you believe he could turn things around.

He told me about his dreams of running an upholstery business. I remember the passion in his voice when he talked about breaking down furniture and putting it back together, giving it new life. To him, it wasn't just a job; it was a craft, an art. And I admired that.

At first, I didn't see the contradictions in his story. I didn't see the cracks in the image I was starting to build in my head. I only saw what I wanted to see—a man with ambition, a man who could complement my life and maybe even add something to it.

But as time went on, I began to notice things that didn't quite add up. Warren had big dreams, but there wasn't much action to back them up. He talked about opening his upholstery shop, but he seemed just as comfortable letting other people pick up the slack in his life. And then there was the inconsistency—the way he could switch from one identity to another, like he was still figuring out who he wanted to be.

Still, I ignored those early signs. I told myself that everyone deserves a chance, that maybe he just needed some time to find his footing. And truthfully, I liked how he looked on my arm. If I could go back to that moment at Jessup, I wonder if I'd see things differently now. Maybe I'd pay closer attention to the cracks instead of just the potential. Or maybe I'd still be drawn to him, despite everything. Because that's the thing about beginnings—they're never as clear as they seem in hindsight.

The Red Flags I Ignored

Warren's words gave me glimpses of his inner turmoil, but I wasn't ready to see them for what they were. He once said to me, *I hate my mother.* Those words were blunt, raw, and unfiltered, and they should've stopped me in my tracks. But they didn't. Instead, I brushed them aside, thinking he was just being honest about his past. Over time, I came to learn that Warren's relationship with his mother wasn't just strained—it was toxic.

He told me stories of his childhood, stories laced with pain and rejection. His mother had her own demons, and those demons left deep scars on Warren. She wasn't nurturing; she wasn't kind. By his account, she was hard, critical, and absent in ways that mattered most. Once, she even pulled me aside and said, *Run. Don't deal with him.* I can still hear the urgency in her voice. It was as if she knew her son better than anyone and wanted to spare me from what she believed was inevitable.

But I didn't listen. I was too wrapped up in what I thought I saw in Warren—the potential, the charm, the dream of who he could become. I justified everything, convincing myself that his struggles with identity were signs of someone trying to find himself. One day, he was a devout Muslim, poring over the Quran. The next, he was considering becoming a Baptist pastor, flipping through a Bible with equal intensity. I saw his search for spiritual grounding as a journey rather than a sign of inner conflict.

Then there was his passion for upholstery. It seemed like a solid dream, one rooted in purpose and skill. He talked about opening his own shop, and for a while, he did. That tiny shop was his pride, his proof that he could build something. But when it burned down, it wasn't just the business that crumbled—it felt like a part of Warren crumbled with it. Even then, I held on to the dream for him, as if my belief in his potential could somehow sustain him.

Defining Moments

Despite the warning signs, we had good times, moments that still make me smile. I can see him now, sitting on my sofa, watching me dance to Adina Howard's *Freak Like Me.* I'd pull on my black-and-white striped stretch pants, channeling all my energy into those performances. I was carefree and alive in those moments, twirling and singing like the world stopped just for us. Warren would sit there, quiet, amused, and maybe a little bewildered by my energy.

But those lighthearted moments were only part of the story. Beneath them, Warren's life was a balancing act between survival and ambition. He flirted with the streets—not fully committing, but not entirely stepping away either. Baltimore in the '90s was a place where hustling was seen as a badge of honor, and Warren seemed drawn to the allure of that life. He'd say, *I hate the system, but I love you,* and then jokingly ask me to keep my correctional officer's uniform on.

At the time, it felt funny, even playful, but now I see it differently. It was a glimpse into Warren's conflict—the push and pull between rebellion and longing, between what he hated and what he wanted. He carried so much unresolved pain and confusion, and instead of confronting it, he wore it like armor, using charm and ambition to mask the chaos within.

Looking back, I see those moments for what they were—pieces of a puzzle I didn't fully understand. Warren wasn't just trying to navigate life after prison; he was wrestling with the ghosts of his past and the weight of his own choices. I was too close to see the full picture then, too caught up in my belief that I could be the steady force he needed.

These memories are complicated—equal parts laughter and heartbreak, light and shadow. They were defining moments not just for Warren, but for me too, shaping how I saw him and how I saw myself. And as much as they taught me about him, they taught me even more about the importance of seeing people for who they are, not just for who we want them to be.

What I'd Tell My Younger Self

If I could go back, I'd sit that younger version of me down and say, *Look deeper. Don't let the surface fool you.* I'd tell her to stop focusing on the potential she thought she saw and start paying attention to the reality right in front of her. The red flags were there, waving as clear as day—the unresolved trauma, the indecision, and the way he depended on others to carry the weight he should have been bearing himself.

I'd remind her that love, no matter how strong, isn't a cure. It can't fix someone who hasn't made the choice to heal. It can't fill the void left by years of pain, neglect, and unaddressed wounds. I'd tell her that ignoring the warning signs doesn't make them go away—it just delays the inevitable heartbreak. And when that heartbreak comes, it's heavier, because you've poured so much of yourself into someone who wasn't ready to receive it.

I'd tell her that it's okay to want to believe in people, but belief alone can't save them. Sometimes, the best thing you can do for yourself—and for them—is to walk away. Because staying often means losing pieces of yourself in the process, pieces that take years to find again.

Discussion Questions for Chapter 1: *In the Beginning*

1. What first impressions in your life have led to significant connections or lessons, for better or worse? How did those impressions shape your decisions?
2. What red flags have you ignored in past relationships or experiences? How did those decisions impact you, and what would you do differently now?
3. How have early moments in a relationship or career set the tone for what followed? Were those patterns healthy, or did they need to be broken?
4. What role does potential play in the way you perceive others? Have you ever been drawn to someone's potential while overlooking their reality?
5. How do your own unresolved past experiences shape the way you connect with others? What steps can you take to address those influences?

Practical Exercises for Chapter 1

1. **Reflection Exercise: The Seeds of Beginnings**
    - Write about a pivotal beginning in your life (e.g., a relationship, job, or decision).
    - Identify the "seeds" planted in that moment. Did they grow into something positive, or did they create challenges you had to overcome?
2. **Red Flag Awareness Worksheet**
    - List at least three times you noticed red flags in a situation but chose to ignore them.
    - For each instance, write what the red flag was, why you ignored it, and what the outcome was.
3. **Journaling Prompt: The Younger Self**
    - Imagine you could speak to your younger self at the start of a significant relationship or decision.
    - Write a letter advising them based on what you've learned since then.
4. **Identity and Potential Mapping**
    - Create a two-column chart. On one side, write the potential you saw in someone (or

something). On the other, write the reality you experienced. Reflect on the gap between the two and how it affected you.

5. **The Roots Assessment**
    - Reflect on the "roots" of your current circumstances. Identify one healthy root you want to nurture and one toxic root you need to address or remove.

Key Terms for Chapter 1

1. **Red Flags** – Early warning signs in relationships, decisions, or situations that indicate potential problems.
2. **Potential vs. Reality** – The distinction between what someone or something could become versus their current state.
3. **Emotional Baggage** – Unresolved issues from the past that influence current behavior and relationships.
4. **Beginnings** – Foundational moments in life that set the trajectory for future experiences.
5. **Resilience** – The ability to recover and grow stronger after challenges or adversity.

6. **Self-Reflection** – The practice of examining your thoughts, feelings, and behaviors to gain deeper self-awareness.
7. **Toxic Relationships** – Connections that drain emotional energy, harm self-esteem, or prevent personal growth.
8. **Pattern Recognition** – The ability to identify recurring behaviors or themes in your life that affect your decisions.

A Call to Reflect

This chapter isn't just my story; it's an invitation for you to reflect on your own. Think about the beginnings in your life—the relationships, decisions, and moments that set your story in motion. What seeds were planted back then, and how have they grown? Have they blossomed into something beautiful, or have they tangled into knots you're still trying to unravel?

Are there red flags you ignored because you wanted so badly to believe in someone or something? Or opportunities you let slip away because you didn't recognize their potential? Beginnings matter. They're not just the starting points; they're the roots of everything we build. And like any roots, they need tending. Some nourish us, while others choke out growth until we have the courage to cut them away.

This is only the first step in a journey of resilience, heartbreak, and redemption. It's about learning to see things clearly, to embrace the lessons hidden in our struggles, and to find strength in the choices we make moving forward.

Through my story, I hope you'll see pieces of your own. I hope it reminds you that it's never too late to rewrite your narrative, to untangle those roots, and to create something better for yourself.

Welcome to *First Lady Blues.* Let's continue this journey together.

Chapter Two

The Roots of the Vine

(John 15:5 - "I am the vine; you are the branches. If you remain in me and I in you, you will bear much fruit; apart from me you can do nothing.")

Family is where everything begins. It's the soil from which we grow, the foundation that shapes us long before we understand its impact. For me, those roots were deeply intertwined with love, tradition, and faith. They stretched across Baltimore, where I spent my formative years, and Amelia County, Virginia, where family ties were nurtured and strengthened. On both sides of my family, I was surrounded by strong values and an unshakable sense of belonging. No matter what life threw at us, we always knew one thing: we had each other.

But not everyone's roots grow in fertile soil. Not everyone has the steadying influence of unconditional love or the safety of a close-knit family. Warren's roots were different—fractured, fragile, and sometimes barely holding on. That stark contrast between his family and mine would become a defining thread in our relationship, shaping how we connected and where we struggled.

A Childhood Full of Connections

Growing up, my family wasn't perfect, but it was everything to me. During the school week, I stayed with my maternal grandparents, who were a pillar of stability in my life. They lived in a modest three-bedroom row house in Baltimore City, but to me, it felt like a mansion because it was always full of love. My grandmother was the heart of our family. Her house was the gathering place, the space where everyone came together.

Holidays were magical. Christmas mornings meant the smell of baked ham wafting through the house and the hum of family laughter echoing in every corner. Thanksgiving dinners were crowded affairs, with people spilling into every room, balancing plates of food and sharing stories that had been told a hundred times but still brought us joy. It didn't matter how small the space was—there was always room for everyone.

Summers were spent in Amelia County, Virginia, where my grandparents' home became the backdrop for a different kind of family bonding. All the grandkids would gather there, working together in the garden, preserving fruits and vegetables, and learning the old ways of making jams and jellies. It was hard work, but it was rewarding. We learned the value of effort and teamwork, and we built memories that tied us to our roots.

What I didn't realize then was that these moments were more than just traditions; they were life lessons. They taught me resilience—the ability to keep going, even when the work was tough. They taught me the importance of staying connected to the people who love you and the value of contributing to something bigger than yourself. And perhaps most importantly, they taught me that family isn't about perfection; it's about showing up for one another, no matter what.

A Contrast in Roots

As I grew older, I began to see how different my upbringing was from Warren's. While my family's roots were anchored in love and community, his were marked by division and isolation. My family taught me that even when there were disagreements, we came back together. We forgave. We celebrated. Warren's family didn't have that same dynamic. The fractures in his relationships with his siblings and mother were deep, and they shaped how he viewed family and trust.

That contrast didn't just highlight where we came from; it shaped how we navigated life together. My instinct was always to build bridges, to bring people together, to create spaces where love could flourish. Warren, on the other hand, often kept people at a distance, creating "family" from those who had shown him kindness, whether or not they were related by blood.

Warren's Roots: A Different Story

Warren's family roots were tangled and fragile, marked by complications and fractures that ran deep. He was one of six siblings, but unity was a concept foreign to their family dynamic. Tensions and unresolved conflicts created walls between them instead of bonds. When his mother passed in 2021, the family's divisions were painfully clear—they didn't even allow Warren to speak at her funeral. For me, someone who grew up in a family where every voice was valued, this level of estrangement was unimaginable.

Warren's approach to family was shaped by survival, not tradition. He often talked about "creating family" with the people who showed him love, regardless of blood ties. It wasn't about who shared his DNA but who offered him kindness, guidance, and support. His definition of family was built on necessity and reciprocity—a stark contrast to my upbringing, where family was a given, not something you pieced together out of life's circumstances.

While I spent weeks planning family cookouts, Christmas dinners, and Thanksgiving feasts, Warren struggled to maintain even the simplest connections with his siblings. They were more like distant acquaintances than family, each living their separate lives with little overlap. This lack of connection left a void that Warren tried to fill by embracing my family as his own.

My uncles became his uncles. My mother treated him like a son. And in many ways, he found in my family what he couldn't find in his own—a sense of belonging. But even then, the scars from his fractured roots lingered.

Breaking Cycles, Building Legacies

The differences in our family dynamics weren't just background details—they were the framework for how we approached life, love, and challenges. I grew up believing in the power of love, forgiveness, and togetherness. Even when my family faced disagreements or tensions, we worked through them. I learned that relationships could be mended, and that healing was always possible when there was a foundation of love.

Warren carried a different story. His family's struggles left him with a fierce sense of independence, a survival instinct honed by years of feeling like he had no one to lean on. That independence made him resourceful, but it also left him with a deep sense of isolation. He referred to himself as a "late bloomer," constantly striving to make up for what he felt was lost time and missed opportunities.

Blending these two worlds—my belief in connection and Warren's instinct for self-preservation—wasn't easy. My natural response to conflict was to forgive, nurture, and create space for reconciliation. Warren's instinct was to retreat, to protect himself by keeping others at a distance. Vulnerability felt like a risk he couldn't afford to take, even with me.

The Legacy of Roots

Looking back, I realize how much our roots influenced the way we moved through life together. Warren's struggle to reconcile with his family taught me that not everyone grows up with the same sense of security and love. It reminded me to never take my own roots for granted and to be intentional about building a legacy of connection and support for my own children.

For Warren, his fractured roots were a source of pain, but they also gave him a unique strength. He learned to navigate life with resilience, finding family where he could and leaning on the few people he trusted. And while it wasn't perfect, it was his way of surviving.

A Reflection

Family, for all its complexity, is where we draw our strength or confront our greatest struggles. Warren's story and mine are proof that our roots shape us, but they don't define us. We can break cycles, mend fractures, and build legacies that look different from what we inherited.

If you're carrying the weight of broken roots, take a moment to reflect: What would breaking the cycle look like for you? How can you redefine family and create the connections you need to thrive?

Your roots might not be perfect, but they can still nourish something beautiful. And even the most tangled vines have the potential to bear fruit when given care and intention.

Let's continue this journey of growth and resilience.

Self-Help Focus: Breaking Generational Cycles

One of the most transformative lessons I've learned is this: understanding where you come from is essential to breaking free from where you don't want to stay. Our family roots hold incredible power. They can be a source of nourishment, grounding us in love and stability, or they can become tangled with pain, neglect, and dysfunction, choking out growth. The key is learning to recognize the patterns within your roots and making the conscious decision to tend them differently.

Breaking generational cycles isn't easy—it requires self-awareness, courage, and often, a willingness to face uncomfortable truths. It starts with looking inward and asking hard questions: *What have I inherited from my family? Are these patterns serving me or holding me back? What can I do differently to create a healthier, stronger legacy for the next generation?*

We all carry something from those who came before us. Some of it is beautiful: resilience, determination, faith. But some of it needs to be left behind: patterns of silence, cycles of trauma, or ways of coping that no longer serve us. Acknowledging both the good and the bad is the first step in rewriting your story.

Ask yourself:

- **What are the strongest values your family instilled in you?** These are the treasures you carry forward.

- **Are there any patterns you've noticed that you want to change for the next generation?** This is where the work begins.
- **How do you define family, and who truly feels like family to you?** This is where healing and growth take root.

Breaking generational cycles isn't just about identifying what's wrong; it's about creating something better. It's about choosing love over fear, forgiveness over bitterness, and connection over isolation. It's about planting seeds for a future where the branches grow stronger, healthier, and more united than the ones before.

Discussion Questions for Chapter 2: The Roots of the Vine

1. How have your family's values shaped your outlook on relationships, resilience, and self-worth? Are these values ones you cherish or ones you've had to redefine?
2. What defining moments from your childhood still influence your decisions and relationships today? How do these moments reflect the roots of your upbringing?
3. What contrasts have you noticed between your family dynamics and those of someone significant

in your life? How have these differences affected your relationship?

4. Have you identified generational cycles within your family that you're determined to break? What steps are you taking to ensure a healthier legacy for future generations?

5. How do you personally define family? Are there people in your life who, while not related by blood, feel like family? Why do they hold that space for you?

Practical Exercises for Chapter 2

1. **Family Tree Analysis:**
    - Create a family tree and annotate it with key traits, values, or challenges you've observed in each generation.
    - Highlight patterns or cycles (positive and negative) that stand out, and reflect on how they've impacted your life.

2. **Letter to Your Roots:**
    - Write a letter to your family roots, expressing gratitude for the strengths they've given you and acknowledging the challenges you've had to overcome.

   - End with a commitment to nurture the legacy you want to create.

3. **Legacy Vision Board:**
   - Create a vision board that represents the family legacy you want to build. Include images, words, or symbols that reflect the values and connections you want to nurture.
4. **Root Reflection Journal Prompt:**
   - Reflect on a family tradition or value that shaped your life. How has it influenced your choices? What parts of it do you want to carry forward, and what parts need to evolve?
5. **Cycle Breaker Action Plan:**
   - Identify one generational cycle you want to break. Write down actionable steps you can take to change this pattern and what success would look like for you.

Key Terms for Chapter 2

1. **Generational Cycles:** Repeating patterns or behaviors passed down within families, such as habits, beliefs, or trauma.

2. **Roots:** The foundational experiences, values, and relationships that shape your identity and worldview.
3. **Family Dynamics:** The patterns of interaction and relationships within a family system.
4. **Legacy:** The values, traditions, and impact you leave for future generations.
5. **Resilience:** The capacity to recover and grow stronger after adversity or challenges.
6. **Family of Choice:** A concept of forming a "family" from supportive, loving connections, regardless of blood relations.
7. **Cycle Breaker:** Someone who recognizes and disrupts harmful generational patterns to create positive change.
8. **Support System:** The network of individuals who provide emotional, practical, and spiritual support in your life.

Concluding Summary

Our roots shape us, but they don't define us. They give us a starting point, not a final destination. As you've seen in this chapter, Warren and I came from two very different vines. My roots were planted in love, forgiveness, and community, while his were tangled with division and survival. Yet, despite those differences, our stories intertwined in ways that pushed us both to grow.

Reflecting on your own roots is a powerful exercise. What parts of your foundation give you strength? What parts need healing or change? Remember, you can't change where you come from, but you can always decide where you're going.

Each choice we make today is a seed for tomorrow. The way we show up for ourselves and our families can change the trajectory of future generations. You have the power to break free from what no longer serves you and to create a legacy that reflects the best of who you are.

Welcome to the journey. Let's continue.

Chapter Three

The Wilderness Years

(Exodus 13:18 - "So God led the people around by the desert road toward the Red Sea.")

Life is full of twists, turns, and unexpected detours. Sometimes, those paths lead us into a wilderness we never imagined—a place of uncertainty, challenge, and change that forces us to confront the depths of who we are. For me, that wilderness began in

1990 and stretched into 1991, a time marked by profound loss, painful lessons, and the sudden, unavoidable necessity to grow up faster than I ever thought possible.

The Back-to-Back Losses

In 1990, I lost my first love, Lucky. He wasn't just my high school sweetheart; he was my rock, my partner, and my anchor in a world that often felt unpredictable. We started dating when I was 15, and by the time we were living together in Glen Burnie, Maryland, Lucky had become my everything. I couldn't imagine life without him.

But life had other plans. Lucky lost his life in a restaurant in Baltimore County. I still remember the moment it happened as clearly as if it were yesterday. Homicide detectives called our house, and though I didn't want to believe it, the look on his mother's face and the sound of her screams confirmed my worst fear. Lucky was gone, another life taken by the streets of Baltimore.

Lucky was more than his struggles, though. He had a heart of gold. Every Christmas, we'd buy toys and sneakers for the kids in Lexington Terrace, a housing project in Baltimore. He cared deeply for others, often putting their needs above his own. But even his kindness and good intentions couldn't shield him from the dangers of the life he was trying to escape.

Barely a year later, in 1991, my stepfather—my second rock—died of cancer. Bo Peep, as we lovingly called him, had been in my life since I was four years old. He wasn't just a stepfather; he was my father in every way that mattered. He taught me stability, generosity, and how to enjoy life's simple pleasures.

Bo Peep was the kind of man who made life feel easy. He bought me my first car when I was just 15, always making sure I had everything I needed. His quiet strength was a constant in my life, and I leaned on him in ways I didn't even realize until he was gone.

The day he died is etched into my memory. That morning, we sat together and talked about coffee—how he was thinking about making a fresh pot, how he always enjoyed the simple things in life. It was a normal, everyday conversation, one I had no idea would be our last. Minutes later, he went to the bathroom, and when he didn't come out, something in me knew. I called out to him, but there was no answer. My heart pounded as I pushed open the door and found him unresponsive. My hands shook as I dialed 911, but deep down, I knew. He was already gone.

That moment shattered me in ways I couldn't have anticipated. Two men who meant the world to me—two pillars of my life—were gone in the span of a year. I was 21 years old, and suddenly, I found myself standing on shaky ground, forced to confront the harsh reality that the people who had always been my safety net were no longer there.

But my father was still present in my life. We had a relationship, one built on visits, shared moments, and drives to see him. He wasn't always front and center, but he was there. He even babysat my oldest son from time to time, stepping in when I needed help. In the midst of loss, his presence was a reminder that not everything was gone—that I still had family, still had people who cared. Even as grief pulled me under, I held onto that.

The Weight of Loss

Losing Lucky and Bo Peep back-to-back felt like a storm I couldn't escape. One moment, I was a young woman with a stable foundation and people to lean on, and the next, I was adrift, struggling to find my footing in a world that felt unbearably empty.

Lucky's death shattered my belief in the idea that good intentions and love were enough to protect the people we care about. Bo Peep's passing, on the other hand, taught me the finality of life and the importance of cherishing every moment with the people we love. Together, their losses forced me to face a truth I wasn't ready for: the people you rely on won't always be there to catch you.

The Lessons in the Wilderness

In the wilderness of grief and uncertainty, I discovered something I didn't know I had—resilience. It didn't come all at once. In the beginning, I felt like I was walking through a fog, unsure of my next steps. But slowly, I began to piece myself back together.

I realized that while Lucky and Bo Peep had always been there to take care of me, their absence was teaching me to stand on my own. Up until then, I hadn't had to navigate life's challenges alone. They had taken care of everything—my bills, my car insurance, even my sense of security. Without them, I was forced to figure out how to handle life on my own terms.

It was during this time that I applied for a job as a correctional officer, a decision that would change the trajectory of my life. The state of Maryland offered tuition assistance, which meant I could continue my education while working, paving the way for my future goals. It wasn't easy, but it was necessary.

Looking back, I see that the losses I endured during those wilderness years were painful, but they also shaped me. They taught me the value of independence, the importance of perseverance, and the power of love—even in the face of unimaginable loss.

Moving Forward

The wilderness years didn't just test me; they transformed me. They forced me to confront my fears, to grow, and to build a life where I could stand strong, even when the people I leaned on were gone.

Lucky's death reminded me to cherish the people I love, while Bo Peep's passing taught me that stability is something you have to create for yourself. Together, their losses pushed me to become the woman I am today—a woman who can navigate life's detours with strength, resilience, and faith.

Life doesn't always go as planned, but it always has lessons to teach. And as hard as those wilderness years were, they prepared me for everything that came next

The Lessons of Loss

Those two losses forced me to confront the kind of life lessons no one feels ready for. Losing Lucky and Bo Peep back-to-back ripped away the safety net I had leaned on for so long. Up until that point, I had lived in a bubble of security, where most of my needs were met without much effort on my part. Lucky and Bo Peep had handled it all—my bills, my car insurance, even making sure I always had nice clothes and shoes. Looking back, I realize how much they had protected me from the weight of responsibility.

But with them gone, reality hit me like a ton of bricks. Suddenly, I had two choices: let the grief consume me or figure out how to build a life where I could stand on my own. Crumbling wasn't an option—not for me, not with everything I wanted for my future. So I made the only choice I could: I chose to rise.

In 1991, I applied for a job as a correctional officer. It wasn't exactly the career path I'd envisioned for myself, but it was the stepping stone I needed. Maryland offered tuition assistance to state employees, and I saw this job as my way to keep moving toward my ultimate goal—law school. That application marked the beginning of my journey toward independence, and while I didn't know it then, it would also become a source of strength and resilience I'd rely on for years to come.

Discovering My Strength

That period of my life taught me something I hadn't fully realized before: I was capable. Smarter, stronger, and more resourceful than I had ever given myself credit for. I learned to trust myself, to make decisions without waiting for someone else to guide me.

Resilience became my foundation—the kind of resilience that doesn't just get you through the day but keeps you moving forward, even when your heart is shattered. Grief doesn't just disappear; it lingers, sometimes whispering doubts and other times screaming them. But I found ways to quiet that voice by leaning into what gave me stability.

Finding Stability in the Storm

During those years, I found stability by focusing on three key areas: education, work, and family. Each became a pillar that helped me rebuild my life one step at a time.

- **School:** Enrolling in classes at Baltimore Community College gave me something to work toward. I juggled coursework with the demands of a 2-to-10 shift as a correctional officer, which wasn't easy, but it gave me a sense of purpose. Education became my anchor, reminding me that every class, every assignment, was a step closer to the future I wanted for myself.
- **Work:** The job in corrections wasn't glamorous, and it wasn't easy, but it gave me financial independence and a sense of control in an otherwise chaotic time. Being able to pay my own bills, handle my responsibilities, and show up for work every day gave me a confidence I hadn't had before.
- **Family:** My mother was my example of perseverance. As a hardworking AT&T employee, she balanced work and home life with grace,

> becoming a role model for me during my toughest moments. My cousins and close girlfriends also became my lifeline. These women, many of whom have been my friends for over 30 years, were like the sisters I never had. They lifted me up, reminding me that I didn't have to navigate this journey alone.

And then there were the family traditions. When my mother passed the torch to me as the family gatherer, it gave me a sense of continuity that I desperately needed. Christmas and Thanksgiving became more than just holidays—they were moments of connection and stability, reminders that even when everything else felt uncertain, family was still there.

The Lessons in Building Stability

What I learned during those wilderness years was that stability doesn't happen by accident—it's something you create. It's in the routines you build, the people you surround yourself with, and the choices you make, even when those choices feel impossibly hard.

I learned that grief and growth can coexist. While I still carried the pain of losing Lucky and Bo Peep, I also carried the lessons they left behind. Lucky taught me to live with compassion and to give to others without expecting anything in return. Bo Peep showed me what it meant to create a foundation of love and security.

I held onto those lessons as I found my footing. Life was different without them, but it was still mine to shape. And with every step forward, I proved to myself that I could rise above the storm and build a future I could be proud of.

Looking Ahead

The wilderness years weren't just about surviving—they were about discovering what I was capable of. Those losses forced me to step into a version of myself I didn't know existed. They taught me that even in the hardest times, we have the power to choose how we move forward.

If you're in your own wilderness season, I want you to know this: you are stronger than you think. Stability is within your reach, even if it feels far away right now. Lean into what grounds you, trust in your ability to rise, and never forget that every detour can lead to a new beginning.

Moments of Growth and Clarity

Looking back, the most significant growth I experienced during those wilderness years came from learning that I could handle it all—school, work, family, and personal growth—without falling apart. It wasn't easy, and there were days when it felt like too much, but every challenge I overcame showed me how capable I really was.

One of the first steps I took was choosing to prioritize what truly mattered. I stopped going to clubs and parties, the distractions that had once felt like an escape, and instead focused my time and energy on building something meaningful. It was a shift in mindset—one that forced me to let go of temporary pleasures and focus on long-term fulfillment.

That decision also opened the door to something new: travel. My cousin Katrina and I started going on cruises and exploring new places together, and those trips became a lifeline for my spirit. Traveling wasn't just about seeing new destinations; it was about rediscovering the beauty of life. Every time I stepped off a plane or cruise ship into a new city or country, I felt a little piece of myself heal. Those adventures reminded me that life could still be beautiful, even after heartbreak and loss.

But the biggest realization of all was how fleeting life can be. Losing Lucky at just 22 and Bo Peep so suddenly drove home a truth that I couldn't ignore: tomorrow isn't promised. Those losses weren't just painful—they were transformative. They pushed me to live differently, to embrace every opportunity, and to hold on tightly to the people I love. I began to cherish every relationship, big or small, and to approach life with a deeper sense of purpose. I wanted to build a future that honored Lucky's compassion and Bo Peep's unwavering support.

Self-Help Focus: Navigating Life's Detours

The wilderness years taught me that detours are not dead ends. They're a different route to the destination, often filled with lessons we wouldn't have learned otherwise. If you're navigating your own detour—a period of loss, uncertainty, or change—know that it's okay to feel lost sometimes. The key is finding ways to keep moving forward.

Here are a few strategies that helped me during my own wilderness years:

1. **Anchor Yourself:**
   Create routines or activities that ground you. Whether it's pursuing education, focusing on work, or embracing family traditions, find stability in the small, consistent things. For me, school and work were anchors that gave me a sense of control during a chaotic time.

2. **Lean on Your Support System:**
   Don't be afraid to rely on the people who lift you up. Family, close friends, or even coworkers can provide the strength and encouragement you need. My cousins and lifelong girlfriends became my emotional safety net, reminding me that I didn't have to navigate this journey alone.

3. **Set Small Goals:**
   In times of uncertainty, having something to work

toward can make all the difference. Start small—whether it's completing a class, saving for a trip, or just showing up for yourself every day. Achieving small goals builds momentum and gives you a sense of purpose.

4. **Practice Gratitude:**
   Even in the hardest moments, there's always something to be grateful for. Focus on the blessings you still have, no matter how small they may seem. Gratitude shifts your perspective, helping you see the light even in dark times.

5. **Rediscover Joy:**
   Don't forget to make space for the things that bring you happiness. For me, travel became a source of joy and healing. Whether it's exploring new places, revisiting an old hobby, or spending time with loved ones, find what fills your soul and lean into it.

Finding Strength in the Detour

What I learned during this chapter of my life is that detours, while challenging, often lead to unexpected growth. They push us to see things differently, to appreciate what we have, and to find strength we didn't know we had. The wilderness years forced me to confront hard truths and make difficult choices, but they also prepared me for the life I wanted to build.

If you're in a season of uncertainty, remember this: you are more resilient than you know. The detour you're on right now might feel like a setback, but it could also be the path to something greater. Keep moving forward, one step at a time, and trust that even the toughest seasons have something valuable to teach you.

Life is precious, fleeting, and beautiful. Let's make the most of it.

Discussion Questions for Chapter 3: The Wilderness Years

1. How have unexpected detours in your life shaped who you are today? Can you identify a moment that felt like a setback but ultimately led to growth?
2. Who or what served as your "anchor" during times of uncertainty or loss? How did that support help you move forward?
3. Reflect on a time when you had to prioritize long-term goals over short-term pleasures. How did that decision impact your journey?
4. What lessons have you learned from people you've lost, and how have those lessons shaped your actions and mindset?

5. If you could give advice to someone navigating their own wilderness years, what would you say to help them stay resilient and hopeful?

Practical Exercises for Chapter 3

1. Create a Detour Map:
    - Draw a timeline of your life, marking significant detours or challenges you've faced. For each, note one lesson you learned or strength you gained. Reflect on how these moments contributed to your growth.
2. **Anchor Journal:**
    - Write about what grounds you during difficult times. Is it family, faith, work, or something else? Identify specific routines, people, or practices that help you stay centered, and brainstorm ways to strengthen those anchors.
3. **Gratitude Practice:**
    - List five things you're grateful for during your current season of life. If you're navigating uncertainty, focus on small blessings that bring light to your days. Make this a weekly habit.

4. **Goal-Setting Exercise:**
   - Break a big goal into smaller, manageable steps. Write out the first three actions you can take and commit to completing them this week. Celebrate each milestone as you work toward your long-term vision.
5. **Legacy Reflection:**
   - Reflect on someone you've lost who made a significant impact on your life. Write a letter to them, sharing how their influence continues to guide you. Consider what part of their legacy you want to carry forward.

Key Terms for Chapter 3

1. **Wilderness Years:** A metaphor for periods of life marked by uncertainty, challenge, or transition that test and shape personal growth.
2. **Detours:** Life's unexpected changes or disruptions that lead to new paths and lessons.
3. **Resilience:** The ability to recover, adapt, and grow stronger in the face of adversity.
4. **Anchor:** A stabilizing force, such as routines, relationships, or values, that provides grounding during difficult times.

5. **Gratitude:** The practice of focusing on and appreciating the positive aspects of life, even in challenging circumstances.
6. **Support System:** A network of people or resources that provide encouragement, guidance, and strength.
7. **Legacy:** The lasting impact or lessons left by someone's life, actions, or memory.
8. **Self-Discovery:** The process of gaining deeper insight into one's values, strengths, and purpose through life experiences.

Concluding Summary

The wilderness years were some of the hardest of my life, but they also prepared me for everything that came after. They taught me resilience, independence, and the importance of creating a life I could be proud of.

As you reflect on your own wilderness moments, remember that detours aren't dead ends. They're opportunities to grow, to learn, and to discover the strength you didn't know you had.

Let's continue the journey together.

Chapter Four

The Labor of Love

(1 Corinthians 15:58 - "Always give yourselves fully to the work of the Lord, because you know that your labor in the Lord is not in vain.")

Life is full of roles, and for me, being a provider and protector has always been at the core of who I am. My labor of love wasn't just about earning a paycheck or fulfilling a duty—it was about building a life for my family. Every late night, early morning, and extra mile was driven by one purpose: to give my children the stability, opportunities, and love they deserved. The challenges were plenty, but every sacrifice felt worth it because it was for them.

Building a Family, One Sacrifice at a Time

As an only child, I always longed for the kind of lively, connected home I'd seen in movies or dreamed up during playtime with my Barbie dolls. My Barbies didn't just have a dream house; they had a full, bustling family to share it with. I wanted to create that reality for myself someday—a house filled with love, laughter, and connection.

When I had my first two sons in 1993 and 1999, that dream began to take shape. Motherhood changed me in ways I couldn't have imagined. The responsibility was immense, but so was the joy. My boys became my world, and everything I did—from the hours I worked to the decisions I made—was to ensure their lives were better than mine had been.

After my youngest biological son was born, I decided that my days of giving birth were behind me, but my desire for a big family didn't go away. That's when foster care entered my life, almost serendipitously. A coworker suggested I sign up, and on a whim, I decided to try it. What started as an experiment quickly became a calling.

My home became a temporary safe haven for children who needed love, structure, and security. Some stayed for a few weeks, others for months, but each one left an imprint on my heart. Then, in 2006, everything changed.

The state placed a six-day-old baby boy in my care. He was tiny, helpless, and absolutely perfect. From the moment I held him, I knew he was meant to be part of my family. It didn't take long for love to take root. By the time he was three years old, I had officially adopted him. That moment marked a new chapter in my life. My family was complete—three boys who were the center of my world and my reason for every sacrifice I made.

Love Through Sacrifice

Building a family wasn't without its challenges, but love gave me the strength to face them head-on. There were times when the demands felt overwhelming—balancing work, school, and parenting required every ounce of energy and patience I had. But every time I looked at my boys, I remembered why I was doing it.

For me, sacrifice wasn't about giving something up; it was about giving something greater. It was about working extra hours to afford private school tuition so they could have opportunities I never did. It was about trading nights out for family dinners, creating traditions that would bind us together. It was about choosing love, even when it was hard, even when I was tired.

A Growing Determination

The adoption of my youngest son solidified something I'd always known deep down: family isn't just about biology. It's about love, commitment, and the willingness to show up every day. My boys didn't just need a mother; they needed someone who believed in them, someone who would fight for their future.

That determination became my driving force. I wanted my boys to grow up in a home where they felt safe and valued, where they could dream big without limits. Every choice I made, every hour I worked, and every sacrifice I offered was a brick in the foundation of the life I was building for them.

And as I watched them grow, I saw that foundation take shape. I saw their confidence, their kindness, and their resilience—qualities that made every struggle worthwhile. They became living proof that love, when paired with hard work and sacrifice, can create something truly beautiful.

Reflections on the Labor of Love

Looking back, I see those sacrifices not as burdens but as blessings. Each one taught me something about myself and about the kind of life I wanted to create for my family. They taught me resilience, patience, and the power of love to transform even the hardest moments into something meaningful.

My labor of love wasn't just about providing—it was about building. Building a home filled with love, laughter, and connection. Building a legacy my boys could be proud of. Building a life that reflected the values I held dear: commitment, sacrifice, and unconditional love.

And I wouldn't trade a single moment of it.

The Career That Shaped Me

My career in criminal justice was more than a job—it was a journey that demanded grit, determination, and a willingness to adapt. I started as a correctional officer, stepping into a role that was both physically and emotionally challenging. It wasn't glamorous, and there were days when the weight of the work felt overwhelming, but it was my entry point into a field that allowed me to build a foundation for my family's future.

While working full-time, I pursued my education relentlessly, earning both my bachelor's and master's degrees in criminal justice. The state of Maryland covered my tuition as long as I stayed in the field, which made the long hours and tough days worthwhile. My education wasn't just for personal achievement—it was a pathway to creating a better life for my boys. Each degree I earned symbolized progress, not just for me, but for my family's future.

After my time in corrections, I transitioned to Clifton T. Perkins Hospital Center, a facility for the criminally insane. It was a role that tested my emotional resilience in ways I hadn't anticipated. The environment was heavy, filled with individuals battling severe mental health issues alongside criminal tendencies. I often left work feeling drained, as if the weight of the job followed me home.

It didn't take long for me to realize that this wasn't the right fit. I needed a balance—something that would allow me to use my skills without sacrificing my mental well-being. That realization led me to parole and probation, a field where I found greater alignment between my professional goals and personal fulfillment. In this role, I could connect with people on a deeper level, helping them navigate the challenges of reentry and accountability.

But for me, work was never just about career advancement. It was about survival and independence. Losing Lucky and Bo Peep at such a young age had taught me a valuable lesson: the only person I could truly rely on was myself. That reality fueled my ambition and shaped my work ethic. I started saving for retirement at 21, determined never to depend on anyone else for financial security.

I worked tirelessly, sometimes juggling two or three jobs at once, because I had a clear vision of the life I wanted to create for my boys. It wasn't easy, but every sacrifice I made was rooted in my promise to myself—to always stand on my own two feet and provide a stable foundation for my family.

Sacrifices for the Next Generation

Raising my boys has been the greatest joy of my life, but it hasn't come without sacrifices. I was determined to give them the best opportunities possible, even if it meant stretching myself thin. Education was a top priority for me, and I made the decision to put all three of my boys in private school. The tuition costs were steep—over $20,000 a year—but I believed the investment was worth it.

To cover those expenses, I often worked part-time jobs in addition to my full-time career. Whether it was picking up shifts on weekends or finding side hustles that fit into my schedule, I found ways to make it work. Complaining wasn't an option for me. My motto was simple: if I wanted something for my family, I would work harder to get it.

In 2000, I achieved another major milestone—I bought my first home. As a single mother, this accomplishment felt monumental. My parents helped with the down payment, but the house was in my name—a testament to my independence and resilience. Owning a home meant more than just having a place to live; it was a symbol of stability for my boys and a tangible reminder of what hard work could achieve.

No matter how tight money got, I found a way to manage. Whether it meant cutting back on luxuries or finding creative ways to stretch a dollar, I refused to let financial stress derail my plans. My focus was always on the bigger picture: creating a life where my boys could thrive and building a legacy they could be proud of.

The Drive Behind the Sacrifices

What kept me going through all the sacrifices was the vision I had for my family. I wanted my boys to grow up knowing that nothing was out of reach if they worked hard enough for it. I wanted them to see that success isn't handed to you—it's earned through perseverance, discipline, and an unwavering belief in your goals.

Every long shift, every sleepless night, and every hard decision was made with them in mind. And when I look at the men they're becoming, I know it was all worth it. The lessons they've learned—about resilience, determination, and love—are the greatest rewards of my labor.

My career and the sacrifices I made weren't just about providing for my family. They were about showing my boys that no matter what life throws at you, you can rise above it. It was about proving to myself that I was capable of building the life I envisioned, even when the odds seemed stacked against me.

The labor of love isn't easy, but it's always worth it. And for me, every step of that journey has been a testament to what's possible when you lead with love, determination, and an unwavering commitment to your family's future.

Moments That Tested Me

One of my most challenging work experiences came later in my career, during my time working for an airline. It was a job that brought its own unique set of demands—dealing with people from all walks of life, often under stressful circumstances. But nothing could have prepared me for the day a passenger handed me her boarding pass, crumpled into a ball.

I politely asked her to unfold it, thinking it was a simple request, but her response was anything but simple. She threw it at me. Stunned, I remained professional, calmly asking her to hand it over properly. That's when the situation escalated. She stormed onto the plane, shouting and spewing racial slurs loud enough for everyone to hear. My face burned with embarrassment and anger, but I knew I couldn't let it show.

The captain was quick to step in, removing her and her husband from the flight. Watching them leave brought some relief, but the encounter left me shaken. I had always prided myself on my professionalism, but this situation tested me in ways I hadn't anticipated.

In that moment, I had a choice. My first instinct was to lash out, to let her know exactly how I felt about her behavior. But something deeper within me took over—a voice that reminded me of what was at stake. My job, my livelihood, and most importantly, my family. I couldn't let one person's ignorance and hostility derail everything I'd worked so hard for.

So, I held my ground with calm and grace. I kept my composure, even when every fiber of my being wanted to react. And in doing so, I reminded myself of an important truth: resilience isn't just about getting through tough times; it's about staying true to yourself in the face of adversity.

That encounter taught me a lesson I carry to this day. There will always be people who try to shake you, who test your patience and your character. But your strength lies in how you respond. It's not about matching their negativity—it's about rising above it.

Self-Help Focus: Finding Balance in Sacrifice

The labor of love isn't just about working hard; it's about navigating life's challenges with intention and balance. Sacrifices are necessary, but they shouldn't come at the cost of your well-being or identity. Here are some strategies that helped me maintain balance during difficult times:

1. **Stay Organized:**
   I've kept a journal since the sixth grade, and it's been a lifesaver. Writing things down—whether it's goals, plans, or even frustrations—helps clear your mind and keeps you focused. Staying organized is about more than managing responsibilities; it's about creating mental space for what matters most.

2. **Prioritize Self-Care:**
   Taking care of yourself isn't a luxury; it's a necessity. Regular doctor's appointments, dental checkups, and even trips to the salon were non-negotiable for me. These moments of self-care not only kept me healthy but also reminded me that I was worth the effort.

3. **Set Boundaries:**
   Sacrifices are part of life, but they shouldn't come at the expense of your peace. Learn to say no when necessary and carve out moments for yourself. Whether it's a quiet evening with a good book or a walk to clear your mind, boundaries are essential for preserving your energy.

4. **Build a Support System:**
   No one can do it all alone. Lean on friends, family, or coworkers who understand your journey. Surrounding yourself with people who lift you up makes the weight of life's challenges feel lighter.

5. **Embrace Gratitude:**
   In the chaos of daily life, it's easy to overlook the blessings. Take a moment each day to focus on what brings you joy—a child's smile, a career milestone, or even a moment of calm. Gratitude shifts your perspective, reminding you of the beauty within the struggle.

A Final Reflection

That experience with the airline passenger wasn't just a difficult moment—it was a defining one. It reinforced what I already knew about resilience: it's about standing firm in who you are, no matter what's thrown your way. Life will always have its challenges, but how you handle them defines your character.

The labor of love isn't always easy. It's about balancing ambition, sacrifice, and self-care while staying true to your values. And as I've learned, it's not just about what you give—it's about how you grow in the process.

Let's keep going. There's more to build, more to learn, and more to celebrate.

Discussion Questions for Chapter 4: The Labor of Love

1. What sacrifices have you made for your career, family, or personal goals? How have those sacrifices shaped your identity and priorities?
2. Can you recall a moment in your life when you were tested—personally or professionally—and how you overcame the challenge? What did you learn about yourself through that experience?
3. How do you define success when it comes to balancing work and family? Has that definition changed over time?
4. What legacy do you want to leave for your children or loved ones, and how are your current efforts contributing to that vision?
5. When was the last time you made time for self-care amid your responsibilities? How can you better prioritize your well-being without compromising your commitments?

Practical Exercises for Chapter 4

1. **Life Balance Assessment:**
   - List your current responsibilities in three categories: work, family, and self-care. Evaluate how much time and energy you

dedicate to each. Are there imbalances? Create a plan to adjust your focus where needed.

2. **Legacy Mapping Exercise:**
   - Write down three lessons or values you want to pass on to your children or loved ones. For each, list specific actions you are currently taking or plan to take to instill those values.
3. **Journaling Prompts for Reflection:**
   - Reflect on a recent challenge and how you handled it. What worked well? What could you have done differently?
   - Write about a time when you felt overwhelmed. What support or strategies helped you navigate that moment?
4. **Self-Care Planner:**
   - Commit to one self-care activity each week for the next month. It can be something simple, like reading a book, taking a walk, or scheduling a spa appointment. Track your activities to ensure consistency.

5. **Gratitude and Vision Exercise:**

    - At the end of each day, write down one thing you're grateful for and one small action you took that contributed to your long-term goals. This practice will keep you focused on both the present and the future.

Key Terms for Chapter 4

1. **Labor of Love:** Work or effort driven by passion, purpose, and dedication, often involving significant personal sacrifice.
2. **Resilience:** The ability to recover from adversity and maintain emotional strength in challenging situations.
3. **Self-Care:** Practices and activities that prioritize personal well-being and mental health.
4. **Boundaries:** Limits set to protect one's time, energy, and peace of mind while managing responsibilities.
5. **Legacy:** The lasting impact of one's actions, values, and contributions on future generations.
6. **Balance:** The equilibrium between work, family, and personal needs, ensuring none are neglected over time.

7. **Support System:** A network of people who provide emotional, practical, or professional assistance during times of need.
8. **Sacrifice:** The act of giving up something valuable to achieve a greater purpose or goal.
9. **Reflection:** The process of looking back on experiences to draw lessons and insights for personal growth.
10. **Gratitude:** Acknowledging and appreciating the positive aspects of life, even during challenging times.

Concluding Summary

The labor of love is never in vain. Every long shift, every late-night study session, and every extra job I took on wasn't just for me—it was for my family, for our future.

As you reflect on your own journey, ask yourself: What sacrifices have shaped who you are? How can you balance ambition with self-care? And most importantly, how can you ensure that your labor leaves a legacy you're proud of?

Let's continue this journey of resilience, purpose, and love.

Chapter Five

Streams in the Desert

(Isaiah 43:19 - "I will make a way in the wilderness and rivers in the desert.")

Life has a way of pulling you back to places you thought you had left behind. Just when you think a chapter is closed, fate has a funny way of showing up, flipping the page when you're not ready—or maybe exactly when you are. For me, that surprise came in the form of Warren, standing at my doorstep during one of the most uncertain and fragile periods in recent memory—the pandemic of 2020. The world was holding its breath, and so was I.

He wasn't empty-handed. He had come bearing supplies: cases of water, toilet paper, paper towels, soap powder, dish liquid—all the things people were hoarding, fighting over in grocery aisles, and panic-buying as if it would save them from the chaos outside. It wasn't the grand, sweeping gesture you'd see in a romance movie, but it hit me differently. It was practical. It was needed. And it wasn't something I expected from him. Warren—the man I had sworn off years ago—was standing in front of me with the essentials of survival in a world that suddenly felt unstable.

I stood frozen for a moment, unsure of what to say. My heart didn't race with excitement. My stomach didn't flutter. Instead, my mind went straight to the warning sirens I had conditioned myself to hear when it came to him. *Not again. Not again.*

I had spent years telling him—and telling myself—that we would never get back together. I had built walls around that part of my heart and convinced myself they were impenetrable. I had made peace with the past, or at least I thought I had. But seeing him there, with his familiar face and that same charm that had drawn me in all those years ago, I felt something I wasn't ready for: hesitation.

My mind raced, flashing through the memories I thought I had buried—the way we ended things back in the '90s, the tears, the betrayal, the emotional scars that still lingered like ghosts in the corners of my mind. Warren had been my weakness once, and I wasn't sure I could survive being that vulnerable again.

And yet, there I was, standing in the doorway, feeling the pull of nostalgia mixed with caution. He wasn't just anyone. He was the man who knew my history, my family, and my heart. But he was also the man who had broken it. I had spent years convincing myself that people don't change, and yet I couldn't help but wonder: Had he?

Had time softened him, matured him, and helped him grow into the man I always wanted him to be? Or was this just another carefully played hand in the game I had sworn I would never play again? The questions swirled in my mind, each one pulling me in a different direction. I didn't know what to believe, and that uncertainty was as terrifying as it was intriguing.

There's something about familiar faces in times of crisis that makes you rethink everything. In a world suddenly filled with fear and isolation, Warren standing on my doorstep wasn't just a surprise—it was a reminder that life isn't always as straightforward as we'd like it to be.

Would I let him back in, both literally and figuratively? Or would I close the door, lock it, and never look back? At that moment, I didn't have the answer. All I knew was that the man who had once been my everything was standing in front of me again, and I had a decision to make.

This wasn't just a knock on the door—it was the start of something I couldn't quite define yet. But as with most things in life, I knew that the only way forward was through. And whether I was ready for it or not, Warren had re-entered my world, bringing with him both questions and possibilities.

Reconnecting in a Time of Isolation

The truth is, Warren had never really left my life—not completely. He had a way of lingering, even when I tried to move on. Over the years, we kept in touch, sometimes more than I wanted. I would find his number lighting up my phone at the most unexpected moments, like he knew exactly when I was vulnerable. When I went through rough patches in my relationships, I would turn to him. Not because he had all the answers, but because he was familiar. When his previous marriage hit rocky ground, he sought comfort in my words, painting himself as the misunderstood husband, the man trying to do right but constantly misunderstood.

There was always something unspoken between us—a connection that never quite snapped, even though it should have. I told myself that it was just history, that you can't easily sever ties with someone who knew your past and your pain. But deep down, I knew the truth: Warren and I had unfinished business, and I had never fully closed the door.

But this time, things felt different. The world wasn't just shifting—it was spinning wildly out of control. The pandemic had changed everything. People were dying by the thousands. Businesses shuttered overnight. Normal life was gone, and we were all scrambling to adjust to a new, uncertain reality. Fear was in the air, not just fear of the virus, but fear of the unknown—of how long this would last and who we would be when it ended. In times like that, people naturally clung to what felt safe and familiar, even if that familiarity came with its own complications.

At the time, I was still working for the airline, but the job had transformed. The once-crowded terminals were ghost towns. Flights that used to carry hundreds of passengers were now carrying five, maybe ten. I remember walking through those nearly empty planes, the sound of my footsteps echoing as if the world itself had fallen silent. The silence was eerie, and the loneliness was suffocating. I had always prided myself on being independent, but the pandemic exposed a truth I hadn't been willing to confront: I needed connection.

Warren became part of my small, quarantined world. My circle was tight—just my immediate family and him. He didn't come with grand gestures or romantic overtures. Instead, he showed up with what I needed: supplies, consistency, and conversation. He dropped off groceries and essentials at my doorstep and stayed to talk, not just about the surface-level stuff, but about life, faith, and the future. He invited me to his church, painting vivid pictures of redemption, new beginnings, and the possibility of us building something meaningful together. He spoke of purpose and growth, and for a moment, I allowed myself to believe in the picture he was creating. Maybe this was our second chance.

A Second Chance or a Well-Planned Trap?

That's the thing about second chances—they make you question everything. I started to wonder: Was this fate? Had we come full circle, finally arriving at the place we were meant to be after all these years? We had always talked about what it would be like if we ever got married. He would be the pastor, and I would be the first lady, leading women's ministries and making sure the church thrived. Maybe, after all the detours and heartaches, the timing was finally right.

But something inside me wouldn't let go of caution. I had learned, painfully, that Warren wasn't always what he seemed. I knew how easily he could make people believe in his image—the charismatic pastor, the man with a plan. But behind the polished exterior was someone who thrived on attention, especially from women.

I saw the signs. I always had. Warren had female friends who would come over for wine nights, bringing him fruit and baked goods. He insisted they were "just friends," but I knew better. He had this way of creating narratives that fit his agenda. He wanted me to believe that women were always chasing him, but the truth was the opposite. He was the one pursuing them, subtly but persistently.

I didn't have to guess—I saw it with my own eyes. I would glance at his phone and see the texts. The messages weren't ambiguous; they were clear invitations. *Would you be interested in being a first lady?* he would ask them, as if he were auditioning women for a role in his life.

I wasn't the only woman he was courting. I was one option among many. He wasn't looking for love—he was looking for someone who fit the image he wanted to project. Someone who could help build the narrative of the successful pastor with a devoted first lady by his side. It wasn't about me. It was about what I could represent.

And still, I stayed.

Why? Because hope is a powerful thing. It can blind you to reality and convince you that change is possible, even when all the evidence points otherwise. I wanted to believe that Warren had changed. I wanted to believe that the man standing on my doorstep with supplies and words of redemption wasn't the same man who had hurt me before. But deep down, I knew that caution wasn't just a voice in my head—it was wisdom earned through years of experience.

I stayed because part of me thought, *maybe this time will be different.* But another part of me knew that staying was just delaying the inevitable. Warren hadn't changed, and neither had the patterns that had defined our relationship from the beginning. I wasn't ready to admit it yet, but the truth was there, waiting for me to face it.

Because second chances are only worth taking when the person on the other side of them has truly done the work to deserve it. And Warren? He was still playing the same game—only this time, I was beginning to see the moves before they happened.

Loneliness Has a Way of Making You Forget

The truth is, I was lonely. I had sworn never to go back to Warren. I had made that promise to myself countless times, repeating it like a mantra every time his name crossed my mind. But promises are funny things—they're easy to make when life is steady, but they start to unravel when you find yourself standing at the intersection of fear and vulnerability. The pandemic had created a vacuum, and into that emptiness, Warren stepped in with the kind of comfort that was hard to resist.

He showed up at a time when the world felt like it was falling apart, when uncertainty was the only certainty, and isolation was a shared experience. He was consistent, reliable even. He didn't come bearing grand gestures; he came with toilet paper, water, and words that promised a different future. And that's where it started—the subtle, dangerous belief that maybe this time things would be different.

I should have left the supplies at the door, thanked him politely, and locked it behind me. But I didn't. Instead, I let the door stay open, just enough for him to slip back into my life. I knew better. I had lived through the hurt, the broken promises, the emotional wreckage he'd left me with in the past. And yet, despite everything I knew, there was still a part of me clinging to the hope that people could change. That time and experience could heal old wounds and transform someone into the person you always believed they could be.

Maybe, just maybe, after nearly 30 years, Warren had become the man I once dreamed he would be—the man who could finally meet me where I was, as an equal, as a partner, as someone who had grown past the lies and the games. Hope has a way of clouding reality. It whispers sweet nothings to your heart while ignoring the warning screams of your gut. I wanted to believe, and for a moment, I did.

But the truth is, I wasn't just hoping Warren had changed—I was hoping I could rewrite our history. I was hoping that if I let him back in, maybe this time the ending would be different. But hope, without change, is just a trap that leads you back to the same pain you were trying to escape.

Self-Help Focus: Building Connection and Community

The pandemic didn't just teach us about social distancing and face masks—it taught us something far deeper about the human need for connection. When the world closes in on you, when fear and uncertainty become your daily companions, you realize how much you depend on others to lift you up or, in some cases, drag you down. Here's what I learned during that time:

1. **Be Cautious with Second Chances:**
   Just because someone re-enters your life during a vulnerable time doesn't mean they belong there permanently. Vulnerability can make you see things through rose-colored glasses, but take a step back and evaluate their intentions. Are they here because

they've changed, or because the timing is convenient for them?

2. **Acts of Kindness Should Be Genuine, Not Transactional:**
   Pay attention to what people expect in return for their generosity. Some acts of kindness come from the heart, and others come with strings attached. Warren showed up with supplies, but part of me knew that his help wasn't purely selfless—it came with expectations. Don't ignore the signs when someone's kindness feels like a transaction.

3. **Loneliness Can Trick You Into Accepting Less Than You Deserve:**
   Being alone is hard, and the world will try to convince you that any company is better than none. But settling for someone who hasn't done the work to grow isn't the solution—it's a trap. I stayed longer than I should have because the weight of loneliness convinced me that maybe this time, the outcome would be different. But settling for a familiar pain only delays your healing.

4. **Build Your Own Community:**
   No one person should be your entire support system. Leaning on just one person—especially someone who has hurt you before—can distort your judgment. Build a community of friends, family, and trusted people who can offer

perspective when you can't see the forest for the trees. They'll remind you of your worth when you forget it.

5. **Trust Your Gut:**
   Intuition is your greatest gift, but it's often the first thing we ignore when we want something badly enough. If something feels off, it probably is. I knew deep down that letting Warren back in was risky. My gut told me to close the door, but I let hope silence that warning. Don't make the same mistake—your gut is usually right.

Final Reflection

Looking back, I see how easy it is to let loneliness blur the lines between hope and reality. I see how much I wanted Warren to be different, not because of who he was, but because of who I needed him to be in that moment. The pandemic made me crave connection, but it also taught me this: not all connections are meant to be reconnected.

Second chances only work when both people have done the work to deserve them. And if one person hasn't grown, the relationship will wither no matter how much hope you pour into it. I learned that the hard way.

But that's the beauty of lessons—they stay with you long after the pain fades. And if you're willing to listen to them, they'll guide you to something better. Because true growth comes not from hoping others will change, but from realizing that *you* have the power to walk away.

Discussion Questions for Chapter 5: Streams in the Desert

(Isaiah 43:19 - "I will make a way in the wilderness and rivers in the desert.")

1. What were the most meaningful or surprising moments during your reconnection with someone from your past? How did they affect your perception of second chances?

2. How did the uncertainty of the pandemic or another crisis in your life reveal who you could truly rely on? Were there any surprises in who showed up—or didn't?

3. In moments of vulnerability, how do you balance the desire for connection with the need to protect yourself from potential harm?

4. Have you ever ignored your intuition when reconnecting with someone, and what was the outcome? What did you learn from that experience?

5. What acts of kindness—either given or received—have transformed your relationships or your perspective on community?

Practical Exercises for Chapter 5

1. **The Connection Inventory:**
    - List the people in your life who have shown up for you in moments of need. Next to each name, write down the specific ways they supported you. Reflect on whether their actions were genuine or transactional. This will help you identify your most reliable support systems.
2. **The Second Chance Checklist:**
    - Create a checklist of key factors to evaluate before giving someone a second chance. Include things like past behavior, current intentions, your intuition, and whether meaningful change is evident. This will help you assess situations with clarity instead of emotion.
3. **Random Acts of Kindness Journal:**
    - For the next seven days, engage in at least one small act of kindness daily—whether it's for a friend, family member, or stranger. At the end of each day, write down how that act affected both you and the recipient. This practice will reinforce the importance of community and connection.

4. **Boundary-Setting Reflection:**
   - Reflect on a time when you let someone back into your life despite your better judgment. Write down what boundaries you would establish if you could go back. Use this exercise to define clear boundaries for future situations.
5. **Faith and Purpose Vision Board:**
   - Create a vision board that represents the values, relationships, and purpose you want to cultivate in your life. Include quotes, images, and words that remind you of what you deserve and inspire you to make decisions that align with your goals.

Key Terms for Chapter 5

1. **Second Chances:** The opportunity to rebuild or revisit a relationship, often dependent on whether meaningful change has occurred.
2. **Vulnerability:** The state of being open to emotional exposure or risk, especially during periods of uncertainty.
3. **Intuition:** The gut feeling or inner voice that guides decisions, often providing valuable insight that logic can't explain.

4. **Transactional Relationships:** Relationships where acts of kindness or support are given with an expectation of something in return.
5. **Genuine Connection:** A relationship based on mutual respect, support, and sincerity, free from hidden motives or conditions.
6. **Community:** A network of people who offer emotional, social, or practical support, especially in times of crisis.
7. **Redemption:** The act of making amends or seeking growth and improvement after past mistakes, often linked to second chances.
8. **Boundaries:** Limits set to protect one's emotional, mental, and physical well-being, ensuring healthy interactions with others.
9. **Acts of Kindness:** Intentional, selfless actions meant to support or uplift others without the expectation of anything in return.
10. **Faith:** A belief in something greater—whether spiritual or personal—that provides guidance and strength during uncertain times.

Concluding Summary

Looking back, I see the pandemic as both a test and a revelation. It revealed who Warren really was, but more importantly, it revealed something about *me.* I was stronger than I realized, but I also had blind spots. I wanted to believe in the fairy tale I had created in my mind for us, even when the reality didn't align.

This chapter of my life taught me that not every stream in the desert is a blessing. Sometimes, it's just an illusion—a mirage of something that looks like relief but disappears the moment you get close enough to touch it.

I should have listened to that voice in my head. The one that said, *Not again.* But sometimes, we have to walk through the lesson to truly learn it.

Let's keep going. There's more to this story.

Chapter Six

The House Built on Sand

(Matthew 7:26 - "But everyone who hears these words of mine and does not put them into practice is like a foolish man who built his house on sand.")

When I look back on my marriage to Warren, I can't help but see the bitter irony in how it all began—a fairy tale wedding, complete with the glitz, the glamour, and the promise of building something beautiful together. I wore the gown of my dreams, and we exchanged vows under the gaze of family and friends. But fairy tales often skip over the hard work it takes to maintain a happy ending, and in real life, the cracks in the foundation don't magically disappear when you say, "I do." If anything, they grow deeper.

Our marriage wasn't built on shared values, honest conversations, or a clear understanding of each other's expectations. It was built on something much more fragile: assumptions, ignored red flags, and a misguided belief that love, by itself, would be enough to bridge the gaps. I thought love could fix what was broken. Spoiler alert: it didn't.

The cracks were there from the start, but like many brides blinded by the glow of the wedding day, I chose not to see them. I was too busy basking in the dream of what I thought we could become. I had spent my childhood imagining that perfect day—the dress, the flowers, the moment I'd walk down the aisle—and now it was happening. I bought a $5,000 wedding gown, sparing no expense on the vision I had carried with me since I was a little girl.

But that gown, which should have been a symbol of joy, became an early warning sign. Warren didn't see it as a celebration of our new life together. He saw it as an unnecessary expense. "You should've bought me a car instead," he said. His words stung, but I dismissed them as a minor disagreement. I told myself that every couple argues over money, that it wasn't a big deal, and that once the wedding was over, everything would fall into place. After all, we were in love, right?

But that comment was more than just a passing complaint—it was a glimpse into our deeper, unspoken differences. While I had been dreaming of the perfect wedding, he had been worrying about practical things like cars and finances. We weren't aligned, and I brushed off that misalignment instead of confronting it. I convinced myself that compromise would come naturally once we settled into married life, but the truth was, compromise is only possible when both people are on the same page. And we weren't.

We both contributed to the wedding costs, and at the time, I saw that as a sign of partnership. In my mind, it meant we were equally invested in our future. But even in that, there were signs of the tensions that would later unravel us. I was meticulously planning every detail—managing the guest list, coordinating with vendors, and ensuring everything went smoothly—while Warren seemed distant, disengaged. He didn't share my enthusiasm, and when I asked for his input, he'd give vague responses or shrug it off entirely.

I chalked it up to stress. Planning a wedding is overwhelming, I told myself. He's probably just overwhelmed, too. But looking back, I realize it wasn't stress. It was a fundamental difference in how we viewed not just the wedding, but the life we were about to build. I saw the wedding as the foundation of something lasting—a symbolic start to a future filled with mutual effort and growth. He saw it as an event, a one-day occasion that wasn't worth the hype or the cost.

And that difference in perspective didn't stop at the wedding. It carried over into our marriage, manifesting in the way we handled money, responsibilities, and communication. What I thought was just a small hiccup at the beginning turned out to be a symptom of a much larger issue: we weren't building on solid ground.

We hadn't talked about our financial goals or how we would manage our money after the wedding. We hadn't discussed how we would handle disagreements or what role our faith would play in our daily lives. We hadn't addressed the red flags that were waving before us, like Warren's tendency to avoid conflict by making decisions without consulting me or his habit of brushing off important conversations with humor or charm. I had assumed that love would smooth over those rough edges. I believed that once we were married, we would naturally grow into the partnership I envisioned.

But love, without communication and shared values, isn't enough. And the more I ignored those early warning signs, the more they grew. What started as a disagreement over a wedding dress became arguments over mortgage payments, credit card debt, and how we prioritized our time and energy. The cracks in our foundation deepened, and by the time I realized how unstable it was, we were already struggling to hold everything together.

If I could go back, I would have done things differently. I would have taken those early disagreements as opportunities to have the hard conversations we avoided. I would have asked him why the cost of the dress bothered him so much and whether it was a sign of deeper financial concerns. I would have demanded that we talk about our expectations for the future—not just the wedding, but the life we were about to build together.

Because the truth is, when you ignore the cracks, they don't go away. They spread, quietly at first, until one day, the entire structure is at risk of collapsing. And by then, it's much harder to fix.

The wedding was supposed to be the beginning of something beautiful, but instead, it was the beginning of a lesson I wouldn't fully understand until much later: a beautiful wedding does not guarantee a beautiful marriage. What guarantees a strong marriage is the foundation you build before you say, "I do." And ours was built on sand.

The Excitement and the Blind Spots

Our early days were filled with excitement—the kind that makes you think you're on the verge of something extraordinary, something unshakable. We traveled to Puerto Rico, Memphis, and Las Vegas, creating memories that felt like snapshots of a life headed in the right direction. There were sun-soaked afternoons on beaches, candlelit dinners, and nights where laughter came easy. It wasn't just about the trips, though—it was about the promise of building something together, a future that seemed just within reach.

Back home, I immersed myself in the church community, driven by the idea that our shared faith would be the glue holding everything together. I threw myself into creating programs like Sunday school and vacation Bible school, filling gaps in the ministry with passion and enthusiasm. I was doing what I thought a good partner—and a potential first lady—should do. On the outside, things looked perfect: a new marriage, shared goals, and what seemed like a common vision for the future.

But beneath the surface, things weren't as steady as they seemed. What looked like a united front was more like two people standing on different ground, trying to convince themselves they were walking in the same direction. The warning signs were subtle at first, easy to dismiss in the glow of newlywed life. But they were there, quietly waiting for their moment to rise.

Before we got married, Warren and I had made a simple agreement: whoever we were seeing before we got together would be cut off, no questions asked. I kept my promise without hesitation. I believed that starting fresh meant letting go of the past. But Warren didn't hold up his end of the deal. I found out he was still entertaining women, brushing it off as harmless fun. "I'm just a trash talker," he said, laughing. "I'm a flirt. It doesn't mean anything."

I believed him because I wanted to. I believed that the vows we made before God would be enough to change him. After all, wasn't marriage supposed to be a new beginning? I thought love could reform habits, that commitment could rewrite behavior. But the thing about building on sand is that it shifts. And eventually, so did he.

The Financial Storm

I thought we had a plan. It wasn't just a hope or a dream—I thought it was a practical blueprint for our life together. Warren would continue pastoring, running his upholstery business, and working his job to help provide for our household. I was used to juggling responsibilities, so I wasn't afraid of the work it would take. But that plan unraveled quickly, starting with a decision Warren made without me: he quit his job.

I didn't find out until after the fact. At first, I told myself, *Okay, we'll adjust.* I had always been good at managing money, making things work even when times were tight. But the problem wasn't just his job—it was the pattern that followed. Warren's lack of financial contribution quickly became a strain on everything. The bills didn't care about our love story. The mortgage needed to be paid, the lights needed to stay on, and tuition checks for my son's private school weren't going to write themselves.

We had agreed early on that one of his small church checks would go toward household expenses, and the other would be his to use. But after a while, even the check for the house wasn't coming in consistently. "Just call the mortgage company," he said one day, casually, as if this was normal. "Tell them they'll get the money when I have it."

I was mortified. That's not how I was raised. In my family, we didn't push off responsibility or make excuses. We made it work, no matter what. If I needed to pick up extra shifts or take on side jobs, I did it. I had been paying my bills on time since I was a teenager with my first paycheck, and the idea of telling someone, *You'll get your money when I have it,* was unfathomable.

But while I was stressing over the bills, Warren was dressing the part of a man who had it all together. He bought new suits, polished shoes, and other luxuries that made him look sharp while I lay awake at night wondering how we'd make it through the month. When he wasn't dipping into what little we had, he was borrowing money from old flames and relying on the generosity of wealthy friends, including two prominent pastors, to bail him out when things got tight. He had his own survival tactics—just not the kind that contributed to the stability of our marriage.

I felt betrayed—not just financially, but emotionally. This wasn't the partnership I had envisioned when we exchanged vows. We hadn't discussed these issues before the wedding because, truthfully, I didn't know they existed. We hadn't done any premarital counseling, and looking back, that was one of our biggest mistakes. As a pastor, Warren should have understood the importance of laying a spiritual and practical foundation, but the pastor who married us didn't require counseling, and we never pushed for it. We skipped the hard conversations about money, responsibilities, and values, thinking love would carry us through.

I wish someone had insisted on it. I wish someone had pulled us aside and said, "Have you talked about what happens if one of you loses a job? What happens if you disagree about spending or saving? Do you understand each other's financial habits and priorities?" Those questions might have forced us to confront the cracks before they widened into the canyon that nearly swallowed us whole.

I believed we were building something beautiful, but you can't build on shaky ground and expect it to last. If we had taken the time to lay everything on the table before saying

"I do," maybe things would have been different. Maybe we would have discovered the gaps early enough to fix them. Or maybe we would have realized that love alone wasn't enough to bridge the distance between us.

But we didn't. And the cost of that oversight wasn't just financial—it was emotional. The strain of carrying the weight of our life on my shoulders chipped away at my trust, my respect, and my ability to see Warren as the partner I needed. The financial storm wasn't just about money—it was about broken promises and the slow erosion of a foundation that was never as solid as I thought.

By the time I realized just how unstable things were, the damage had already been done.

Cracks in the Foundation

The financial issues between Warren and me weren't just about money—they became a symbol of everything we hadn't talked about, everything we hadn't built properly from the start. His expectations of marriage and mine couldn't have been more different. I wanted a partner who would lead, protect, and provide—a man who would build a life *with* me, not depend *on* me. He, on the other hand, wanted a wife who would carry him while he figured things out. I had signed up for a partnership; he was content with something far less equal.

One night, after yet another argument about our roles in the marriage, he looked at me and said, "You're becoming too masculine." He didn't mean it as a joke or a passing comment—it was meant to wound, to make me question the strength I had developed in the face of his inaction. I laughed bitterly and shot back, "Well, you're becoming ******." I wasn't trying to be cruel, but I had reached my breaking point. I was exhausted—working two jobs, flying extra trips to cover the bills, managing the household, and still trying to be a mother, all while he sat comfortably chasing dreams without a plan or urgency.

The imbalance in our relationship was suffocating, and it eroded our connection piece by piece. I wanted someone who would share the burden, not place it squarely on my shoulders. But Warren didn't see it that way. He was caught up in ideas and promises, while I was stuck dealing with the practical reality of keeping the lights on and the mortgage paid. I wasn't just tired—I was drained emotionally, physically, and spiritually.

The intimacy between us faded like a candle burning down to its wick. It wasn't something I could force or fake anymore. I didn't want him to touch me, and I didn't want to be touched by someone who couldn't fulfill the role of the husband he had promised to be. Intimacy requires more than physical presence—it requires trust, security, and mutual respect. And by then, all of that was gone.

Lessons from the Sand

It's easy to look back and think, *I should have seen it coming.* The warning signs weren't hidden. They were right there, but love can blind you. It convinces you that things will get better, that people will grow, that the problems you see today will be solved tomorrow. I ignored things I shouldn't have ignored. I heard things I shouldn't have brushed off. But here's what I've learned—lessons I wish I'd known before I said "I do" on shaky ground.

1. **Don't Skip the Hard Conversations:** Marital counseling isn't just a box to check off on your wedding to-do list—it's a necessity. You *have* to have those uncomfortable, raw conversations about finances, family expectations, responsibilities, and what happens when life doesn't go according to plan. We didn't do that. We skipped over the hard stuff, assuming that love would fill in the gaps. But love, without honest communication, isn't enough.

2. **Red Flags Don't Disappear After the Wedding:** If you see something that doesn't sit right before marriage, don't convince yourself it will magically disappear after the vows. It won't. In fact, it will probably get worse. The warning signs I saw before the wedding—his financial irresponsibility, his tendency to dismiss important conversations—were the same things that caused the biggest problems

later. I believed that marriage would mature him, but the truth is, marriage only magnifies what's already there.

3. **Don't Marry Potential:**
   I didn't just marry Warren—I married the version of him I had created in my head. I married the idea of what I thought he could become if he just put in the effort. But potential isn't a guarantee. Don't marry someone's potential; marry who they are today. If they haven't shown you the ability to follow through on their promises before marriage, don't expect them to change afterward.

4. **Protect Yourself Financially:**
   Love is beautiful, but it won't pay the bills. Make sure both partners have a financial plan and are contributing to the household. Don't make the mistake of assuming that "love will figure it out." It won't. Warren's lack of financial contribution didn't just put a strain on our bank account—it put a strain on our marriage. Financial stress will test any relationship, and if both people aren't equally invested in making things work, the foundation will crumble.

5. **Trust Your Instincts:**
   Deep down, I knew something was off long before things fell apart. My gut told me that the foundation

> we were building wasn't solid, but I ignored it. I convinced myself that love was enough to fix the cracks. But here's the truth: your instincts are there to protect you. If something doesn't feel right, trust that feeling. It's better to confront the discomfort early than to deal with the damage later.

Looking back, I realize that the biggest lesson wasn't about what Warren did or didn't do—it was about what I allowed myself to accept. I allowed myself to believe in potential over reality. I allowed myself to carry the weight of a marriage that wasn't built to last. But I also learned that mistakes don't define you—what you do after them does.

I walked away from that marriage with more than just scars. I walked away with wisdom, resilience, and the understanding that the right partnership doesn't make you question your worth—it reinforces it. And that's the kind of love I now know I deserve.

Discussion Questions for Chapter 6: The House Built on Sand

(Matthew 7:26 - "But everyone who hears these words of mine and does not put them into practice is like a foolish man who built his house on sand.")

1. What were the red flags in a past or current relationship that you ignored, hoping things would

improve? What was the outcome, and how would you handle it differently today?

2. How do you define "partnership" in a relationship, and what specific qualities or actions do you expect from a partner? Have those expectations ever been unmet, and how did that affect the relationship?

3. In what ways have financial stress or differences in money management impacted your relationships or personal life? What lessons did you take away from those experiences?

4. Have you ever relied on someone's potential instead of accepting their reality? How did that belief influence your decisions, and what did you learn from it?

5. What role does self-reliance play in your relationships, and how do you balance supporting a partner without carrying the entire load yourself?

Practical Exercises for Chapter 6

1. **Red Flag Reflection:**

    - Write down three red flags you've ignored in past relationships. Reflect on why you ignored them and what lessons you've learned. Then, list three ways you will address or confront red flags in future relationships.

2. **Financial Alignment Exercise:**
   - Sit down with your current or hypothetical partner and have a money conversation. Discuss savings goals, debt management, and household contributions. Create a financial plan together and identify any areas of misalignment that need resolution.
3. **The Reality vs. Potential Chart:**
   - Create two columns: one labeled "What I See" and the other labeled "What I Hope For." Write down the qualities of a partner (or past partner) that represent their current reality in the first column, and what you hoped they would become in the second column. Reflect on whether marrying potential is a pattern for you and brainstorm ways to avoid it.
4. **Healthy Boundary-Setting:**
   - Reflect on moments where you felt the weight of a relationship was uneven. Identify the boundaries you need to set moving forward to ensure a healthier balance. Write

down ways you will communicate those boundaries clearly.

5. **Instinct Tracker:**
   - Keep a "gut feelings" journal for two weeks. Write down any moments where your instincts speak up—whether it's about a decision, a person, or a situation. Track the outcomes to strengthen your trust in your intuition.

Key Terms for Chapter 6

1. **Foundation:** The core elements upon which a relationship is built, including trust, communication, shared values, and financial stability.
2. **Red Flags:** Warning signs or behaviors that indicate potential problems in a relationship or situation.
3. **Financial Partnership:** The shared responsibility of managing money and making financial decisions within a relationship.
4. **Marrying Potential:** Committing to someone based on who you believe they can become, rather than who they are in the present.

5. **Self-Reliance:** The ability to depend on oneself for emotional, financial, and practical stability, even within a relationship.
6. **Emotional Labor:** The mental and emotional effort involved in supporting and managing a relationship, often unevenly distributed.
7. **Boundary Setting:** Establishing limits to protect one's well-being and maintain balance in relationships.
8. **Gut Instincts:** The intuitive feelings or immediate reactions that guide decisions, often before logic fully kicks in.
9. **Financial Misalignment:** Differences in how partners manage or prioritize money, which can lead to conflict or instability.
10. **Partnership:** A relationship based on mutual respect, effort, and collaboration, where both individuals contribute meaningfully to its success.

Concluding Summary

Our house wasn't built on rock. It was built on hopes, dreams, and ignored warning signs. And like any house built on sand, it couldn't withstand the storms that came. But this chapter of my life taught me the importance of building strong foundations—in relationships, in finances, and in life.

For anyone reading this: take the time to build your foundation the right way. Have the hard conversations. Set the boundaries. And never, ever ignore the cracks.

Let's keep going—because the storm is just getting started.

Chapter Seven

Clouds Without Rain

(Jude 1:12 - "They are clouds without rain, blown along by the wind.")

Marriage, they say, is a union built on trust, love, and commitment—a partnership where two people hold each other up, weathering life's storms together. But when the foundation starts to crack, when promises go unfulfilled and dreams are deferred, it feels like standing under a cloud that promises rain but never delivers. The earth beneath you dries up, barren and lifeless, while you wait for something—anything—to nourish the relationship back to life. That's what my marriage to Warren had become: a house filled with expectations that never quite materialized, leaving me to battle the storm on my own.

From the outside, we looked like the picture of success. People admired us, and why wouldn't they? I was a flight attendant, seamlessly juggling work, raising my boys, and maintaining a busy household. Warren was a pastor, someone who carried the weight of the pulpit and had a respected community presence. Together, we fit the image of a power couple: polished, composed, and seemingly unstoppable. But appearances, I've learned, are often the most deceptive of illusions.

Behind closed doors, we were fighting silent wars—wars that didn't erupt into shouting matches but simmered beneath the surface, wearing us down little by little. Each unmet promise was like a brick removed from the walls of our home, creating spaces where doubt, resentment, and disappointment crept in. He would make commitments—to get a new job, to contribute more to the household, to be the partner I needed—but those promises dissolved as quickly as they were made. Every time he failed to follow through, the tension between us grew heavier.

The arguments weren't always explosive. In fact, it was often the quiet disappointment that cut the deepest. There were nights when we sat across the dinner table, barely speaking, each of us lost in our own thoughts. I'd replay conversations in my head, dissecting his words, trying to understand why we kept circling the same issues without resolution. He, on the other hand, seemed content to brush things under the rug, as if ignoring them would make them disappear.

But they didn't disappear. Unspoken frustrations have a way of festering, and soon, even the smallest disagreements felt like battles. We argued over finances, over time management, over his lack of follow-through. I wanted him to be the man I could lean on, the man who would share the load with me. But instead, I found myself carrying more and more while he drifted further into his own world of aspirations without action.

The tension wasn't just about money or household responsibilities—it was about trust. Trust that he would do what he said he'd do. Trust that he valued our partnership as much as I did. But with each broken promise, that trust eroded, leaving cracks in the foundation that neither of us could repair. I stopped expecting him to change, but that didn't make the disappointment any easier to bear.

Marriage isn't just about love; it's about accountability. It's about knowing that when one partner stumbles, the other will be there to help steady the ship. But I couldn't steady the ship alone—not when I felt like I was the only one rowing. The more I tried to hold things together, the more isolated I felt. The weight of carrying the marriage on my back was suffocating, and eventually, I realized that love wasn't enough to save us.

The image of a power couple is only as strong as the reality behind it. And the reality of our marriage was that we were two people moving in opposite directions. I was fighting to hold onto something I believed in, while he was living in the potential of what he *might* become—one day, someday, if things ever lined up perfectly. But life doesn't give you perfect conditions. It gives you challenges, tests, and opportunities to rise to the occasion. And Warren wasn't rising. He was standing still.

I learned that when a partner repeatedly fails to show up for the relationship, it doesn't just create distance—it creates doubt. Doubt about your worth, your choices, and your future. I began to question whether I was asking too much or if I was simply expecting the bare minimum: commitment, honesty, and shared effort. The answer became painfully clear: I wasn't asking for too much. I was asking the wrong person.

Standing under that cloud, waiting for the rain that never came, I realized that some storms aren't meant to be weathered—they're meant to teach you when it's time to walk away. And in the end, that's exactly what I did. Because a marriage built on sand will eventually collapse, no matter how hard you try to hold it up. And I was done holding it up alone.

Small Signs, Big Problems

The warning signs were always there, quietly flickering in the background, waiting for me to acknowledge them. But like many people in love, I ignored them. At first, they seemed small—just quirks of Warren's personality that I could manage or fix. His tendency to gravitate toward the wrong crowd was something I told myself was temporary, a part of him that would fade as we settled into married life. But it didn't fade—it intensified.

After church on Sundays, instead of coming home to unwind with me and the family, Warren would head straight to the neighborhood bar where he grew up. He'd sit with old friends, reliving past glory days over rounds of drinks, swapping stories like he hadn't moved on from that part of his life. The pastor I had married—the man who stood in the pulpit preaching about faith and discipline—was the same man sitting in a dimly lit bar, drowning in nostalgia and alcohol.

I should've been more alarmed. The signs had been there long before we exchanged vows. During our engagement, I witnessed one of those glaring red flags at a community event where I was running a pop-up shop selling women's dresses. Warren tagged along to support me, but what should have been a supportive outing turned into something else entirely. There were alcoholic slushies being served, and Warren drank them like they were water. Before I knew it, he was drunk—stumbling, laughing, and dancing wildly in the middle of the park. I had introduced him to people as "Pastor Savage," but there he was, swirling around like the life of the party, making a spectacle of himself. I was mortified.

The embarrassment cut deeper than just the public scene. It was about what it symbolized—a deeper problem I had been too afraid to confront. I knew Warren had a history with alcohol. He had a DWI in his past, but I had convinced myself that was behind him, just a chapter he'd closed before meeting me. The drunk pop-up shop moment should have shattered that illusion, but I was still clinging to the hope that it was a one-time mistake. That's the thing about ignoring red flags, though—they don't disappear just because you close your eyes. They stay, they grow, and eventually, they force you to face the truth you've been avoiding.

Living with Unfulfilled Promises

Warren wasn't just battling alcohol; he was at war with himself. His struggles weren't limited to one bad habit—they were woven into his entire life. He had big dreams, and on the surface, they were impressive: earning his PhD, building a thriving church, and creating a comfortable life for us. But dreams without action are just fantasies, and Warren's actions rarely aligned with his words.

He talked about success with the confidence of someone who believed it was already within reach, but he didn't do the work to back it up. When he enrolled in school, I thought it was a step in the right direction, a sign of progress. But instead of applying himself, he asked me to type his papers and paid classmates to help him with assignments. His idea of progress was delegating the hard work to others, hoping he could ride the wave of their effort.

I wanted to believe in him. I wanted to believe that the man who stood before the congregation every Sunday, leading prayers and inspiring others, could become the man he envisioned for himself. But the reality was different. His promises of financial stability were empty words, and the burden of keeping us afloat fell squarely on my shoulders. I was paying for the mortgage, the utilities, and my son's private school tuition. My job as a flight attendant wasn't just supporting my boys—it was keeping our entire household together while Warren's financial contributions dwindled to nearly nothing.

One of the hardest moments came when I discovered that Warren had accumulated $3,000 in parking tickets. It wasn't just the tickets that upset me—it was the expectation that I would fix it. Without hesitation, he expected me to pay them, like it was my job to clean up the mess. But this time, I refused. I had always paid my own bills, worked extra shifts when needed, and made sacrifices to ensure that the lights stayed on and the bills were paid. I expected the same level of responsibility from him. When I told him no, it triggered a firestorm of arguments that seemed to happen daily.

"You're supposed to have my back," he would say, throwing those words at me like they were a weapon designed to guilt me into submission. But how could I have his back when he wasn't willing to stand on his own two feet? I had supported him in every way I could—emotionally, financially, spiritually—but there's only so much support you can give someone who refuses to help themselves. Warren wasn't just leaning on me; he was leaning so hard that I was on the verge of collapse.

Our arguments weren't just about money. They were about broken trust, unmet expectations, and the resentment that builds when one person carries more than their share of the weight. I resented him for making promises he couldn't keep. I resented him for seeing me as a safety net instead of a partner. And most of all, I resented myself for believing that love could fix what clearly needed more than love—it needed accountability, responsibility, and growth, none of which Warren was willing to offer.

That's the thing about living with unfulfilled promises: they don't just disappoint you—they break you. They chip away at your confidence, your faith, and your sense of stability until you're left questioning whether the person you fell in love with was ever real. I wanted Warren to succeed, but I realized that wanting it for him wasn't enough. He had to want it for himself, and that was the one thing I couldn't give him.

My Job Became My Sanctuary

Work wasn't just a paycheck—it was my escape. My job as a flight attendant became the one place where I could breathe without feeling the weight of Warren's broken promises and the tension suffocating our home. When the arguments grew too loud, when the emotional distance between us felt like a chasm I couldn't cross, I'd pick up a flight and leave. Within hours, I could be in Costa Rica, Los Angeles, or some other city where the chaos of home felt like a distant memory.

But no matter how far I traveled, the weight of my marriage came with me. In the quiet of hotel rooms, where the hum of air conditioning was the only sound, I would sit and think about the promises we made when we stood before God, family, and friends. I'd replay the moments when love had seemed enough and wonder how we had gone from *forever* to *barely holding on.* I blamed myself sometimes. Maybe if I had been more patient, maybe if I had pushed less or given more grace, things could have been different. But deep down, I knew better. You can't fix what the other person refuses to acknowledge is broken.

Warren's refusal to seek help was one of the most devastating parts of our struggle. I suggested counseling—multiple times, from different angles. I told him that seeking help didn't make him weak, that it wasn't a reflection of failure but a chance for growth. I even reached out to resources within his Methodist denomination, thinking he might respond better to help from within the church. But Warren was firm. "Pastors don't need outside help," he'd say. "I can handle it on my own." But he couldn't.

Instead of seeking professional guidance, he turned to alcohol and the company of people who enabled his worst habits. They validated him, reassured him that he didn't need to change, and encouraged him to stay exactly as he was. There was no accountability, no one holding him responsible for his actions. The man who had stood at the altar promising to be a leader and a protector was now a man hiding from his own reflection.

I tried to pull him back. I tried to bring us back. I initiated countless conversations, desperate to find some way to salvage what was left of our marriage. But those conversations rarely ended the way I hoped. More often than not, they turned into arguments—heated, circular debates where no progress was made. I felt like I was fighting alone, trying to save a marriage he had already quietly abandoned.

A Tipping Point

By early 2024, the cracks we had been patching over for years had widened into gaping fractures. The financial strain was constant. The emotional disconnect between us was a silent, suffocating presence. And Warren's behavior—the drinking, the denial, the lack of effort—had created a distance that no amount of love or forgiveness could bridge. I was exhausted from fighting, tired of hoping he would finally see what was slipping away.

But the tipping point—the moment when everything truly fell apart—came in August 2024, when our youngest son, "Baby Boy," passed away. There's no pain like losing a child. It's a grief that doesn't just break you—it shatters you. And when you're already standing on shaky ground, grief has a way of accelerating the inevitable. For us, it highlighted every unresolved issue, every unspoken resentment, and every promise Warren had failed to keep.

I remember the days following Baby Boy's passing in fragments. The numbness, the tears, the weight in my chest that made it hard to breathe. I wanted Warren to be my partner in grief, to hold me up when I couldn't stand on my own. But instead, the distance between us grew wider. We grieved differently—he retreated further into himself, while

I was desperate for connection, for some sign that we could face this tragedy together. But that sign never came.

The truth is, the cracks in our foundation weren't new. They had been forming long before we said, "I do." We had simply been too blinded by love—or too afraid of failure—to confront them. But grief doesn't give you the luxury of ignoring what's broken. It magnifies it. It forces you to see the flaws you once tried to overlook. And for us, there was no way to go back. The weight of losing our son was too much for a marriage already on the verge of collapse.

I wish I could say we found a way to heal together, but we didn't. Warren and I were standing in the same storm, but we were facing it from opposite sides. And when the storm cleared, all that was left was the realization that we couldn't rebuild what had already been washed away.

A New Beginning

Looking back, I understand now that some endings are necessary, even if they're painful. Our marriage wasn't built to withstand the pressures of life's biggest tests because we never built it on a strong foundation to begin with. But from that crumbled foundation, I found something else—strength. Strength to walk away, strength to rebuild my life on my own terms, and strength to learn from the mistakes I once thought would define me.

Because even when the rain doesn't come, there's still a chance to plant something new. And this time, I'm building on solid ground.

Self-Help Focus: Preparing for Life's Challenges

The lessons I learned from this chapter of my life weren't just hard-earned—they were transformative. They forced me to confront my fears, my blind spots, and the parts of me that wanted to believe love could fix anything. But the truth is, love alone isn't enough. When you see the clouds forming, don't sit back and hope for clear skies. Take action before the storm becomes unmanageable, before the damage becomes irreversible. Waiting only makes the fall harder.

Here are the strategies that helped me survive the storm, even when my marriage couldn't be saved. They are lessons I now carry into every part of my life, and they're what I want you to carry with you, too.

1. Recognize the Signs Early

Red flags don't wave themselves in your face—they often start as subtle hints, little cracks that you can easily dismiss as "not that serious." But what seems minor today could be the root of something catastrophic tomorrow. Warren's small acts of financial irresponsibility, his reliance on others to do the work, and his refusal to address our problems didn't seem like deal breakers at first. I told myself they were temporary, manageable. But small cracks grow, and ignoring them only gives them time to spread.

The lesson? Don't minimize your instincts. If something feels off—whether it's a broken promise, a pattern of neglect, or a subtle shift in your partner's behavior—pay attention. Those signs are rarely wrong.

2. Set Boundaries and Stick to Them

One of the hardest things to learn is that love does not mean limitless sacrifice. Boundaries aren't about pushing someone away; they're about protecting your peace, your mental health, and your future. When Warren accumulated $3,000 in parking tickets and expected me to cover them, I said no. Not because I didn't want to help my husband, but because constantly cleaning up his messes would have destroyed me. Setting that boundary wasn't just about money—it was about respect. It was about saying, "I will not allow your choices to become my burden."

The lesson? Boundaries teach people how to treat you. Don't be afraid to set them. If someone doesn't respect your boundaries, that's a sign they don't respect your value.

3. Seek Help, Even If It's on Your Own

I begged Warren to go to counseling, to talk to someone, to face our issues with the help of a neutral third party. But he wouldn't do it. He believed that as a pastor, asking for help was a sign of weakness. That belief trapped him, but I refused to let it trap me. I went to counseling alone, and it saved me. My therapist became a lifeline, helping me untangle my emotions, understand my triggers, and recognize that I didn't have to bear the weight of the marriage by myself.

The lesson? Even if your partner won't seek help, *you can.* Therapy isn't just for couples—it's for anyone who needs clarity, healing, and a plan to move forward. Don't wait for someone else to be ready.

4. Don't Isolate Yourself

One of the biggest dangers of a toxic relationship is isolation. Whether intentional or unintentional, it's easy to withdraw when you're overwhelmed by emotional and financial stress. I've always been independent, but during the hardest parts of my marriage, I leaned on my support system like never before. My mother, my girlfriends, and my mentors were my lifelines. They listened without judgment, offered advice when I asked for it, and reminded me of my worth when I forgot.

The lesson? Surround yourself with people who uplift you. Isolation breeds hopelessness, but connection builds resilience. Don't be afraid to ask for help or simply let someone sit with you in your pain.

5. Know When to Let Go

Perhaps the hardest lesson of all was understanding that strength isn't just found in staying—it's found in knowing when to leave. For years, I told myself that leaving would mean I had failed. That walking away from my marriage would be a betrayal of the vows I took. But here's what I learned: staying in something that's breaking you isn't noble, it's destructive. There's a point where holding on does more damage than letting go, and recognizing that point is a form of strength, not weakness.

I reached that point in 2024, when grief and unresolved issues collided and left nothing to hold onto. I knew then that I had given everything I could, but a relationship cannot survive on the efforts of one person alone. Leaving wasn't just about ending the marriage—it was about reclaiming my life.

The lesson? Letting go isn't giving up; it's making space for something better. It's recognizing that your future deserves more than a relationship built on broken promises.

These lessons shaped who I am today, and I wouldn't trade them for anything. Yes, they came from pain, but pain often brings the most valuable wisdom. If you find yourself standing under a cloud that won't deliver rain, don't stand there waiting for the storm to pass. Take control. Set boundaries, seek help, build your support system, and when necessary, let go. Because the only thing worse than a storm is staying in one when you have the power to walk away.

Discussion Questions for Chapter 7: Clouds Without Rain

(Jude 1:12 - "They are clouds without rain, blown along by the wind.")

1. What red flags or early warning signs have you ignored in past relationships, hoping they would improve over time? What were the consequences of ignoring them?
2. Have you ever felt like you were carrying most of the emotional or financial weight in a relationship? How did you cope, and what did you learn from that experience?
3. What role does unfulfilled potential play in relationships, and how can you distinguish between supporting a partner's growth and enabling their stagnation?
4. Reflect on a time when you relied on external appearances to maintain a relationship's image. How did that impact your emotional well-being?
5. When have you experienced a "tipping point" moment in a relationship or situation, and how did it influence your decision to stay or walk away?

Practical Exercises for Chapter 7

1. **Red Flag Inventory:**
    - Write down five "red flags" you've encountered in relationships or life situations. Next to each one, note how you responded at the time and what you would do differently now. Reflect on what ignoring those signs cost you emotionally or practically.
2. **Emotional Balance Check:**
    - Create a list of the responsibilities (emotional, financial, or practical) you currently handle in a relationship. Are they evenly distributed, or are you carrying more than your fair share? Identify any areas where boundaries or adjustments are needed.
3. **Rain or Mirage Exercise:**
    - Think about a promise someone made to you that was never fulfilled. Was the promise realistic, or was it based on potential and wishful thinking? Write down how you can avoid falling into the same trap of waiting for "rain" that never comes.

4. **Gut-Check Journaling:**
    - For one week, keep a journal of any moments where your intuition tells you something is wrong or off in your relationship or life. Write down how you feel in the moment and what action you took (or didn't take). At the end of the week, review your entries and reflect on the patterns.
5. **Boundary Reset Activity:**
    - Write a list of boundaries you want to set (or reset) in your relationships. Next to each boundary, write down why it's important and how you'll communicate it to the other person. Practice role-playing the conversation if necessary.

Key Terms for Chapter 7

1. **Red Flags:** Early warning signs or behaviors that indicate potential problems in a relationship or situation.
2. **Emotional Labor:** The mental and emotional effort invested in maintaining relationships, often unevenly distributed.
3. **Unfulfilled Potential:** The gap between who someone is and who they could be, often used as justification for staying in difficult relationships.

4. **Tipping Point:** A critical moment where small issues accumulate, leading to a major decision or change.
5. **Boundary Setting:** The act of establishing limits to protect your emotional, mental, or physical well-being.
6. **False Promises:** Commitments made without follow-through, leading to unmet expectations.
7. **Emotional Disconnect:** The breakdown of intimacy, trust, and connection between partners.
8. **Support System:** A network of friends, family, or mentors who provide guidance, encouragement, and accountability.
9. **Intuition (Gut Feeling):** The instinctive sense that something is right or wrong, often based on subtle cues and experiences.
10. **Emotional Resilience:** The ability to navigate challenges, recover from setbacks, and maintain well-being during difficult times.

Concluding Summary

My marriage to Warren taught me that love isn't enough to sustain a relationship when the foundation is built on sand. Trust, shared values, and consistent actions are what hold things together. Without them, even the most beautiful house will fall.

This chapter is a reminder that we can't control others, but we can control how we respond. We can set boundaries, seek help, and make choices that prioritize our well-being.

As I reflect on this period of my life, I see the lessons clearly: don't wait for the rain. If the clouds show signs of trouble, take shelter before the storm hits. And if you find yourself in the storm, remember—you have the strength to weather it and rebuild when the skies clear.

Let's keep going—the hardest part is still to come.

Chapter Eight

The Tempest

(Psalm 107:29 - "He stilled the storm to a whisper; the waves of the sea were hushed.")

The Storm That Changed Everything

Life has a way of hitting you hardest when you least expect it. One moment, you're going through the motions, believing you've already seen your share of heartbreak, and then, without warning, a storm comes that makes everything before it feel like a drizzle.

For me, that storm arrived on a day that should have been unremarkable. A normal Saturday. The kind of day that blends into the rest. The sun was shining, and I had just returned home from a three-day work trip. There was nothing about that morning—nothing at all—that hinted at the devastation waiting for me inside.

I called out my son's name, expecting the usual—his voice carrying from his room, his laughter bouncing off the walls, the sound of his feet moving toward me. But silence greeted me instead. At first, I wasn't alarmed. I knew he had a full day planned—helping my aunt at the church, getting a haircut. He was always on the go. But something tugged at me. A whisper of unease. His bed was made—too neatly, almost staged. That whisper grew louder, settling in my chest like a weight I couldn't shake.

I went through the motions, distracting myself with the small tasks of homecoming—unpacking, sorting the mail, cleaning out my lunchbox from my trip. But the quiet clung to the air, thick and unnatural. Then, as I headed downstairs, my world came to a standstill.

He was there. Lying on my bed. Still.

For a split second, I told myself he was just sleeping. That he would stir when I called his name again. That he would open his eyes, flash that grin, and make me feel ridiculous for worrying. But he didn't. I stepped closer, my heartbeat drowning out every other sound.

I reached out—his arm was cold.

The weight in my chest turned to crushing pressure. My knees buckled, and the room blurred around me. I must have screamed, but I don't remember it. I must have called 911, but I don't recall dialing. What I do remember, with agonizing clarity, was the moment the truth settled in—my baby was gone.

Paramedics arrived, but they weren't rushing. There was no urgency in their movements. No frantic attempts at resuscitation. Just questions. Too many questions—What time did you last see him? Was he sick? Had he been upset? I could barely form words, let alone answer. The police followed, then crisis managers, then neighbors who stood in hushed disbelief. My house, once filled with warmth, had become a cold, unfamiliar space.

The Hardest Call

And then, I had to do the unthinkable.

I had to tell my mother.

But I couldn't do it myself. **I couldn't find the words, couldn't force them past the lump in my throat.** How do you say something so impossible? How do you tell your mother that her grandchild is gone?

I called my cousin instead. **I asked her to go get my mother, to bring her to me.** I needed her close, but I needed time. Time for the coroner to arrive. Time for them to take my son's body from the house. **Time to shield my mother from the image that would haunt me for the rest of my life.**

I don't remember what I said when she finally arrived. **I only remember how it felt.**

The kind of pain that doesn't just hurt—it consumes. **It rips through your body, claws at your chest, steals the breath from your lungs.** It is beyond grief. It is devastation. **And once it takes hold, it never truly lets go.**

They say there is no pain like losing a child. I had heard those words before, but until that moment, I had never understood their weight.

The days that followed were not days at all—just stretches of time blurred together by exhaustion and an emptiness I couldn't escape. I was surrounded by people, but I had never felt more alone.

I couldn't eat. I couldn't sleep. Every room in my house felt like a mausoleum, haunted by memories that had once been a source of joy. I saw him everywhere. The hallway where he used to come running, the kitchen where he stood sneaking snacks, the framed photos lining the walls—each one now a painful reminder of what had been stolen from me.

And then, there was *his* room.

I couldn't bring myself to step inside. I would stand at the doorway, staring at the bed still made the way he left it, his clothes folded neatly, his cologne lingering faintly in the air. I wanted to freeze time, to preserve everything exactly as it was—because moving anything felt like erasing him.

Grief is a thief. It takes your strength, your sanity, your will to function. It makes every normal thing feel impossible. I wasn't sure how I would survive it, or if I even *wanted* to survive it.

But I wasn't the only one drowning.

My family grieved. My mother grieved. My closest friends grieved. And Warren—he grieved, but in a way that would eventually break everything apart.

Grief isn't just about loss. It reveals. It amplifies. It takes whatever is already weak and makes it weaker. And what was already broken in my marriage? The fractures that had been hidden beneath the surface?

They were about to shatter completely.

The Breaking Point

I had expected Warren to be my rock. After all, he was a pastor. A man of faith. If anyone should have known how to navigate this kind of pain, it should have been him. But grief doesn't just reveal who we are—it magnifies it. It strips away pretense and lays every flaw, every weakness, every unresolved wound bare. And our marriage? It had already been fractured. Losing our son didn't create the cracks; it only deepened them.

Instead of leaning on each other, we drifted apart. It was like we were stranded in the same storm, but each of us in separate lifeboats, unable—or unwilling—to reach for the other. While I fought to keep my head above water, Warren let himself sink.

He drank.

Every night. Every day. He found a reason. A justification. A way to escape.

I would watch him pour a drink as soon as he walked in the door, see the way his hands gripped the glass tighter than he had ever held me in those final months. He wasn't just numbing the pain—he was numbing himself to *everything.* I would talk, and he wouldn't hear me. I would cry, and he wouldn't reach for me. The man who once swore before God to love and protect me had become a stranger in our own home.

And then, the unthinkable happened.

It was only days after our son's funeral. We had checked into a hotel, desperate for a change of scenery, some kind of escape from the unbearable weight of our house. But the weight followed us. It clung to our skin, settled into the silence between us.

And then, in the middle of an argument about money—because what else was new?—he said the words that would push me over the edge.

"You're the reason he's gone."

The room went quiet. **My breath caught in my chest.**

I don't remember thinking. I don't remember deciding to react. **I just remember pushing him—hard.** And in the next instant, his hand came down—not across my face, but directly into the braces in my mouth.

A sharp, searing pain shot through me, metal cutting into the inside of my lips. My mouth filled with the metallic taste of blood, but it was nothing compared to the shock that rippled through my body.

Warren had never hit me before. Not once. **But that moment changed everything.**

I didn't reach for my cheek. **I felt the sting, the ache in my mouth, the slow realization of what had just happened.** And in that instant, something inside me shattered.

This wasn't just grief. This wasn't just a marriage in crisis. This was the moment I knew—I couldn't stay.

I grabbed my things and walked out, **my vision blurred with tears, my heart pounding in my chest.**

By the time I made it back home, I knew something had changed forever. **And this time, there was no going back.**

The Isolation of Pain

One of the hardest parts of grieving was the unexpected loneliness.

I had always believed that in times of great sorrow, the church would be there. After all, I had been there for *them*—teaching Bible school, organizing vacation Bible school, running programs for the children, showing up when others needed help. I had poured into that church, into that community, into those people.

But when it was my turn? The church doors stayed closed.

At first, I thought it was just shock. That maybe people didn't know what to say. But then, the silence stretched longer and longer. The phone calls stopped. The check-ins faded.

And then I found out the truth.

They had been *told* not to contact me.

Warren's administration—the same people I had worshipped beside, prayed with, served alongside—had decided that we needed "space." That I needed "time."

But space was the *last* thing I needed.

I needed presence. Warmth. People. I needed someone to sit with me in my grief, to remind me that I wasn't alone. Instead, I felt abandoned by the very community I had given so much to.

And that's when the real questions started creeping in.

I questioned my faith.

I questioned my purpose.

I questioned my *role* as First Lady, as a wife, as a woman who had spent years believing that if you give, you will receive. That if you serve, you will be served. That if you love, you will be loved in return.

I couldn't stay in the house where my son had died. I physically *couldn't.* Every room felt suffocating. Every hallway held memories that threatened to crush me. So I left. I stayed with family, trying to find refuge in places that didn't hold the same unbearable weight.

I prayed constantly.

Sometimes out of faith.

Sometimes out of sheer *desperation.*

I begged God to show me a way through, to take away the pain, to give me some kind of sign that this suffering had a purpose. But for the longest time, all I got in return was silence.

And that silence was deafening.

The Long Road to Healing

Grief doesn't disappear. It doesn't have an expiration date. It doesn't follow a schedule. It lingers in the background, sometimes quiet, sometimes roaring, but always present. I used to believe that time alone could heal all wounds. That if I just pushed forward, if I stayed busy, if I kept moving, the pain would eventually fade. But grief doesn't work like that. You don't get over it—you learn to live with it.

For me, the first step toward healing came through therapy.

It took six months before I could even step back into my house without feeling like I was suffocating. The walls held too many memories. The silence screamed at me. Every corner of that house reminded me of what I had lost, of the boy who had filled those rooms with laughter, with life. I thought about selling it, about leaving it behind and starting fresh somewhere else. But deep down, I knew that no matter where I went, grief would follow.

So instead, I tried to reclaim my space.

I painted the walls. I bought new furniture. I changed the layout of the rooms, hoping that shifting my surroundings would somehow shift the way I felt inside. But grief isn't something you can paint over. It isn't something you can hide behind new furniture or new routines.

I had to sit with it.

I had to feel it.

I had to learn how to carry it, not as a burden that crushed me, but as a part of my story that shaped me. The weight of it never fully lifted, but I learned how to bear it, how to carry it with grace instead of resistance.

And slowly, day by day, I started to find small moments of peace—not in forgetting, but in remembering without breaking.

Lessons from the Storm

If there's one thing I've learned from this season of my life, it's that storms don't come to destroy you—they come to reveal what was already weak.

Losing my son didn't just test my strength; it exposed every fault line in my life. It showed me what was real and what was an illusion. It forced me to confront things I had spent years avoiding.

Here's what I know now:

1. **You Can't Ignore the Cracks.**
   If something is broken—whether it's a relationship, a foundation, or your own mental health—face it. Ignoring it doesn't make it disappear; it just allows the damage to spread. The signs were always there in my marriage, in Warren's choices, in my own exhaustion. But I didn't want to see them. Looking back, I wish I had been braver sooner.

2. **Grief Demands to Be Felt.**
   You can try to outrun it. You can drown it in distractions. You can pretend it doesn't exist. But grief is patient—it will wait. And when it catches up with you, it will demand to be felt. The only way to heal is to allow yourself to break first. I learned that grief is not something to fight; it's something to

surrender to. Only then can you begin to move through it.

3. **Not Everyone Will Show Up for You.**
   Some people will surprise you with their love and support. Others will disappear the moment things get too heavy. I spent too much time grieving the people who left instead of appreciating the ones who stayed. If I could go back, I would tell myself to stop chasing after those who didn't care enough to be there and to pour my energy into those who did.

4. **You Are Stronger Than You Think.**
   There were days I didn't think I would survive this. Nights when I thought the grief would swallow me whole. But I did survive. The pain didn't go away, but I learned how to carry it. I learned that strength isn't about never falling—it's about getting back up, even when you don't want to. Even when it feels impossible.

5. **Healing Is a Choice.**
   It doesn't happen on its own. You have to fight for it. You have to wake up every day and choose to keep going. Choose to get out of bed. Choose to take care of yourself. Choose to believe that there is still life beyond the pain.

And one day, without even realizing it, you wake up and find that the storm has passed. The grief is still there, but it no longer controls you. The pain still lingers, but it no longer defines you.

You survived.

And that is something no storm can take away.

The Calm After the Storm?

The waves of grief never fully recede. They don't disappear like footprints washed away by the tide. Instead, they settle into the rhythm of your life—sometimes crashing, sometimes quiet, but always present.

For a long time, I felt like I was drowning, caught in an undertow that refused to let me go. Every breath was heavy, every step uncertain. The weight of loss, betrayal, and heartbreak clung to me like a second skin. I was standing in the wreckage of my life, staring at the pieces, wondering if I had the strength to rebuild.

But here's the thing about storms: they don't last forever.

My marriage didn't survive the tempest, but I did.

And survival, as I learned, is not just about making it through the night—it's about finding the courage to step forward into the morning.

At first, I didn't know what that step looked like. The life I had built, the identity I had poured myself into as a wife, a mother, a First Lady—it all felt shattered. I wasn't sure who I was outside of the roles I had played for so long. But piece by piece, I started rebuilding. Not just my life, but myself.

I threw myself into healing—not just the surface-level, "I'm fine" kind of healing, but the deep, soul-searching, uncomfortable kind. Therapy became my safe space. Prayer became my anchor. I allowed myself to break, to cry, to rage, and then, slowly, to hope.

Because in the midst of it all, even when I questioned, even when I doubted, even when everything I knew had crumbled—God had never left me.

There were moments when I wasn't sure I could hear Him. Moments when the silence felt deafening, when my prayers felt empty, when I begged for answers that never came. But looking back, I see it now—He was there. In the people who showed up. In the quiet whispers of strength when I wanted to give up. In the resilience I didn't think I had, but somehow, I kept finding.

And somehow, even in the middle of the storm, even when I thought the waves would pull me under, I knew:

This wasn't the end of my story.

It was just the beginning of something new.

I had been broken, but I wasn't defeated. I had lost, but I wasn't lost. I had walked through the fire, but I was still standing.

And now, I was ready to rise.

Discussion Questions for the Reader

1. **The Weight of Unexpected Loss**
   - Have you ever experienced a moment that changed your life in an instant? How did you process it, and what emotions surfaced in the days that followed?
2. **Grief and Relationships**
   - How has grief affected your relationships with others? Did it bring you closer to some people and push you away from others? Why do you think that happened?
3. **Coping Mechanisms: Healthy vs. Destructive**
   - When faced with overwhelming pain, how do you cope? Do you turn inward, seek distractions, or lean on others? Are there coping habits you want to change?

4. **The Loneliness of Grief**
    - Have you ever felt unsupported in a moment when you needed people the most? How did you handle that experience, and what did it teach you about the people around you?
5. **Finding Strength in the Storm**
    - Think of a time when you faced loss, heartbreak, or an unexpected storm in life. What was one thing that helped you keep going, even on the hardest days?

Practical Exercises

1. Writing a Letter to Your Loss

- Whether it's a person, a relationship, or a dream that didn't come to pass, take a moment to write a letter to what you lost. Be honest about your emotions—anger, sadness, love, or gratitude. You don't have to send it or share it, but sometimes, putting feelings into words can bring clarity and healing.

2. Identifying Your Grief Triggers

- Make a list of things that trigger your grief—dates, places, songs, certain conversations. Next to each one, write down a strategy for how you can handle those moments when they come.

3. The Support Circle Reflection

- Create two lists: one with the people who have truly shown up for you in hard times, and another with those who disappointed or distanced themselves. What patterns do you notice? How can you build stronger relationships with those who genuinely support you?

4. Grounding Techniques for Overwhelming Moments

- When grief feels unbearable, grounding techniques can help. Try:
    - **5-4-3-2-1 Method:** Name 5 things you see, 4 things you feel, 3 things you hear, 2 things you smell, and 1 thing you taste.
    - **Deep Breathing Exercise:** Inhale for 4 counts, hold for 4 counts, exhale for 4 counts. Repeat.
    - **Create a Safe Space:** Picture a place (real or imaginary) where you feel at peace. When overwhelmed, close your eyes and mentally "go" there.

5. Rebuilding After the Storm: A Personal Action Plan

- What's one small, realistic step you can take toward healing? It could be making a therapy appointment, reaching out to a trusted friend, starting a new routine, or creating a memory tribute. Write it down, and commit to taking that step within the next week.

Key Terms List

1. **Grief Journey** – The unique, personal process of mourning and healing after a loss.
2. **Survivor's Guilt** – The feeling of guilt that can accompany losing someone, wondering why you were left behind.
3. **Emotional Numbing** – The act of shutting down emotionally to avoid pain.
4. **Disenfranchised Grief** – Mourning a loss that isn't widely acknowledged or understood by others.
5. **Crisis of Faith** – A period of questioning one's spiritual beliefs after experiencing deep suffering.
6. **Trauma Response** – The way the mind and body react to sudden emotional distress.

7. **Complicated Grief** – A prolonged, intense form of grief that interferes with daily life.
8. **Triggers** – Situations, places, or memories that bring back intense emotions tied to loss.
9. **Resilience** – The ability to adapt and grow stronger after experiencing hardships.
10. **Healing Rituals** – Personal or spiritual practices that help in processing grief, such as prayer, journaling, lighting a candle, or visiting a special place.

Final Thoughts

Grief is not something you "get over." It's something you learn to live with. **You are allowed to mourn, to feel lost, to question everything—but you are also allowed to heal.**

The storm may have changed you, but it did not break you.

You are still standing. You are still here.

And that means your story is not over yet.

Chapter Nine

Beauty from Ashes

(Isaiah 61:3 - "To bestow on them a crown of beauty instead of ashes.")

The Breaking Point

There comes a time when you stop fighting for what was and start fighting for what could be. For me, that moment wasn't a dramatic explosion—it was a quiet, unshakable realization. I simply couldn't afford Warren anymore—not emotionally, not spiritually, and certainly not financially. After my son passed, whatever glue had been holding us together completely disintegrated. The grief was unbearable, but what made it worse was realizing I was carrying it alone.

Warren had checked out. Not just of our marriage, but of life, of responsibility, of everything that should have mattered. I was drowning in loss, and he was busy making sure I was still showing up for *his* needs while he neglected mine. The bills were piling up, the weight of the mortgage sat squarely on my shoulders, and when I needed a partner, I found myself alone. Again.

The moment that sealed it for me was a regular Tuesday afternoon—no thunderclap, no dramatic background music, just reality smacking me in the face. I had finally made the difficult decision to sell the house I had lived in for 25 years—the home where I raised my children, the space filled with both joy and pain. I had brought two men over to give me an estimate, walking through the yard, assessing what it would take to move on, to start fresh.

Then Warren pulled up. The look on his face was a mixture of confusion and anger. "You're selling the house?" he asked.

I didn't hesitate. "Probably."

And just like that, everything unraveled. His voice rose, his frustration bubbling over. "Where the **** am I supposed to go?"

That's when it hit me—**he had never planned for anything.** He had never considered that this marriage required work, that life required accountability. He expected me to figure things out, to carry the weight, to keep us afloat. He expected me to stay.

For years, I had been the problem solver, the one making sure things got done. And for years, I had waited for him to take his place beside me, to contribute, to step up. But he never did. **And I finally realized that I didn't have to wait for him to be ready. I was ready.** I was done.

I had been telling him for weeks—we needed to find a place, start fresh, build something different. But Warren never heard me, because in his mind, I wasn't leaving. In his mind, I would always be the safety net.

That day, I told him:
If you're not going to help me carry this, then you have to go.

The Separation

October 24, 2024—our official separation date. The day I put an end to the exhausting cycle of hoping, trying, fixing, and waiting.

Warren packed up his things—well, some of them. He didn't take everything because, in his mind, maybe this wasn't permanent. Maybe I would change my mind. Maybe, at some point, I would step in and save him again.

But I didn't. I couldn't.

A month later, life threw us both into forced reflection. **Within 24 hours, we were both in separate accidents.** I broke my wrist roller skating, and Warren totaled his van and fractured his leg. It felt like the universe itself was demanding we slow down, sit in the weight of our choices.

I remember lying in bed, wrist aching, heart still heavy with grief, and asking God, *What are you trying to tell me?*

Then, just as I was settling into this new life without Warren, the phone rang.

Warren had suffered a brain aneurysm. He was in the hospital, conscious, but weak, with a tube draining blood from his head.

A Different Kind of Goodbye

The irony was impossible to ignore. After all the fights, all the disappointments, all the moments I told myself I was done, I still found myself by his bedside.

Because despite everything, I still cared.

Because despite everything, I still wanted him to be okay.

But standing in that hospital room, I knew something else, too. **Being there didn't mean going back.**

At some point, Warren woke up. He looked at me, eyes heavy with pain, maybe regret, maybe something else neither of us could put into words. I told him, "If you need to come back to the house, you're welcome."

But even as I said it, I knew the truth—**he didn't want to come back, and I didn't need him to.**

He looked at me, his voice quieter than I had ever heard it, and said:

"I'm just gonna work on myself. And you work on yourself."

And in that moment, I let him go.

Breaking, Then Becoming

Losing my son shattered me. Losing my husband set me free.

For the first time in what felt like forever, I was standing alone—not as someone's wife, not as someone's mother, not as the First Lady of a church, but as **me.** And that realization was both terrifying and liberating. I had spent so much of my life taking care of everyone else—nurturing my children, supporting my husband, tending to a congregation that didn't always pour back into me. Somewhere along the way, I had forgotten what it meant to take care of myself.

I had poured myself out until I was empty, running on fumes for so long that I didn't even recognize the weight I had been carrying. And when it all crumbled—when grief knocked me to my knees and loss stripped away every title and every role—I was forced to ask a question I had been avoiding for years:

Who am I when I'm not carrying someone else?

Walking Away to Walk into Myself

Resigning from my positions in the church was one of the hardest things I ever had to do. Those kids? They *loved* me. Every Sunday, they would leave their parents' pews and come sit next to me. To them, I was their First Lady, even if the church refused to acknowledge the title. They trusted me. They confided in me. They saw me.

Walking away from them felt like another loss, another grieving process. But I knew I couldn't keep pouring from an empty cup. **I needed to step back so I could find myself again.**

So I started visiting other churches—not searching for a title, but searching for peace. I volunteered in different ways, no longer tied to the expectations of a congregation that had once turned its back on me. I got involved with my neighborhood association, donating to local kids' basketball teams, helping with community programs, finding new ways to serve.

And that's when it hit me. **I didn't need a title to be a leader.** I didn't need to be the First Lady of a church to make an impact. My purpose wasn't confined to one place, one role, or one relationship.

I had spent years defining myself by the roles I played in other people's lives. But what if there was more for me?

Finding Beauty in the Ruins

For the longest time, I thought healing meant going back to what I had lost. I thought that if I could just fix what was broken, if I could just piece everything back together, then I would feel whole again.

But healing isn't about going back. **Healing is about moving forward.** It's about taking the ashes of what was and finding something beautiful in what remains.

I had spent years giving to people who didn't know how to pour back into me. **I had surrounded myself with takers.** And now, for the first time, I was learning how to pour into *myself*.

Healing didn't happen in a single moment. There was no grand revelation, no perfect epiphany that made everything clear. **It came in small, quiet moments.**

It came in morning walks when I allowed myself to breathe.
It came in journaling, writing down my thoughts without filtering them.
It came in reconnecting with old friends, laughing in a way I hadn't in years.
It came in finally taking time to just *be.*

And in the stillness, I realized something: **I had spent so long chasing love that I had forgotten to love myself.**

Lessons from the Ashes

If I could go back and speak to the woman I was when this storm began, I would tell her:

1. **You don't have to set yourself on fire to keep others warm.**
   Love should never cost you your peace, your stability, or your sanity. If it does, it's not love—it's sacrifice, and not the kind that builds, but the kind that drains.

2. **Let go of people who are not growing with you.**
   It's okay to love someone and still know that they're not meant to be in your life. Some people

are seasonal, and trying to force them into your forever will only stunt your growth.

3. **Your healing is your responsibility.**
   No one is coming to save you. No one can do the work for you. The life you want, the peace you crave, the joy you deserve—you have to build it for yourself.

4. **God will replace what you lost with something greater.**
   It might not look like what you expected, but trust that **beauty will come from the ashes.** Every loss, every tear, every heartbreak is making room for something new.

5. **You are allowed to start over.**
   Your past does not define you. Your pain does not have to be your final chapter. There is life on the other side of heartbreak—if you're brave enough to step into it.

Moving Forward

When I look back at everything I've been through, I don't see a woman who was broken. **I see a woman who was refined.**

The storm didn't destroy me—it revealed me. It burned away everything that wasn't meant for me, cleared the path for something new.

And now, as I stand on the other side, **stronger, wiser, and freer than I've ever been**, I know one thing for certain:

This isn't the end of my story. It's the beginning of something new.

Self-Help Focus: Rebuilding After Loss

Rebuilding After Loss: Carrying the Love, Not Just the Pain

Rebuilding after loss isn't about forgetting—it's about learning how to carry your memories without letting them weigh you down. It's about honoring the past while creating space for the future. I had to learn that healing didn't mean leaving my son behind or erasing the love I once had for Warren. **It meant choosing to live fully, even in the face of heartbreak.**

Grief will try to convince you that if you smile again, if you find joy again, if you dare to move forward, then you are somehow betraying what you lost. **But that's a lie.** Healing isn't an act of forgetting—it's an act of remembrance. **It's choosing to take the love with you and leave the pain behind.**

If you're on your own healing journey, here are some strategies that helped me find my way forward:

1. Create a Healing Plan: Small Steps Toward Wholeness

When you're in the depths of grief, thinking about the future can feel impossible. The weight of it can make even getting out of bed seem like a monumental task. That's why I had to break my healing down into **small, intentional steps**—things I could focus on daily to move forward, one moment at a time.

- **Start with what you can control.** Maybe it's making your bed, stepping outside for fresh air, or journaling for five minutes.
- **Set simple, achievable goals.** It could be as small as drinking enough water, calling a friend, or reading a scripture that brings comfort.
- **Acknowledge progress, no matter how small.** Healing isn't about giant leaps—it's about tiny steps that, over time, rebuild your strength.

I learned that I didn't need to have it all figured out. I just needed to take the next right step.

2. Surround Yourself with Life-Givers: Find Your People

Loss has a way of exposing the people in your life. Some will disappear when things get hard. Others will surprise you by showing up in ways you never expected. **Pay attention to the difference.**

I had to be intentional about surrounding myself with people who poured life into me instead of draining me. **The ones who didn't judge my grief but sat in it with me.** The ones who reminded me of my strength when I couldn't see it myself.

- **Find your encouragers.** The friends who check in, the family members who show up, the mentors who speak life into you.
- **Distance yourself from those who drain you.** Some people only take. If they make you feel guilty for grieving or pressure you to "move on" before you're ready, they're not the support you need.
- **Lean into your faith community.** If your past spiritual circle failed you, seek out new spaces where you feel seen, supported, and uplifted.

I learned that healing isn't meant to be done alone. **Find your life-givers, and let them walk beside you.**

3. Rediscover Yourself: Who Are You Now?

Loss changes you. The version of me that existed before my son passed, before my marriage ended, before the storm came—**she's not the same woman standing here today.** And that's okay.

For so long, my identity was tied to being a wife, a mother, a First Lady. **But when those roles shifted, I had to ask myself: Who am I now?**

- **Explore new passions.** Try things you never made time for before—painting, writing, traveling, learning something new.
- **Revisit old joys.** What did you love before life got complicated? What hobbies, dreams, or interests did you put on hold?
- **Give yourself permission to change.** You don't have to be who you were before. Let yourself evolve.

I realized that rediscovering myself wasn't selfish—it was necessary. **I wasn't just surviving. I was learning how to live again.**

4. Let Go of Guilt: Healing Doesn't Mean You Stop Loving

One of the hardest parts of healing is letting go of the guilt that whispers, "If you move on, you're forgetting them." That's not true.

Healing doesn't mean you stop loving those you lost. **It means you honor them by living fully.**

- **Talk to them.** I still have conversations with my son in my heart. I tell him about my day, about the things I wish he could see.
- **Honor their memory in your own way.** Some people start foundations, create traditions, or find quiet personal ways to keep their loved one's spirit alive.
- **Forgive yourself.** Grief comes with "what ifs." What if I had done something differently? What if I had seen the signs? But healing requires grace—for yourself and for the things you couldn't control.

I had to remind myself that my son **wouldn't want me to live in sorrow.** He would want me to laugh, to grow, to find joy again. And that's exactly what I choose to do.

5. Embrace the Journey: Healing Is Not Linear

Some days, I woke up feeling strong. Other days, I felt like I was drowning all over again. That's the nature of healing. **It's not a straight line—it's a winding path with highs and lows.**

- **Let yourself feel.** There will be moments when grief hits you out of nowhere. Don't push it away. Let it come.
- **Give yourself grace.** There's no timeline for healing. Take it day by day.

- **Celebrate progress.** Even if you still have hard days, recognize how far you've come.

I had to accept that healing wasn't about getting "over" anything. **It was about learning to carry the love forward, without letting the pain define me.**

Moving Forward with Purpose

There will always be moments when grief sneaks up on me—holidays, birthdays, the random quiet moments when I least expect it. But now, I know how to navigate it.

I don't run from my pain. I carry it with strength. **I carry my son with me in every moment, in every step forward.**

Rebuilding after loss isn't about forgetting—it's about choosing to live again, fully and unapologetically. **Not just because life moves on, but because I deserve to move forward with it.**

And so do you.

Discussion Questions for the Reader

1. **Rebuilding After Devastation**
    - Think about a time when life as you knew it completely changed. What was the first step

you took toward rebuilding? What made that moment possible?

2. **Unexpected Sources of Healing**
   - Sometimes, healing comes from places we least expect. Have you ever had an experience, person, or moment that helped you heal in a way you didn't anticipate?
3. **Faith in the Midst of Pain**
   - Has hardship ever made you question your faith or your beliefs? What helped you either strengthen or redefine your spirituality in that season?
4. **Lessons from the Fire**
   - After going through loss, heartbreak, or failure, what did you learn about yourself that you may not have learned otherwise?
5. **Redefining Strength**
   - Society often tells us that strength means pushing through pain without breaking. How has your understanding of strength evolved through your struggles?

Practical Exercises

1. The Healing Timeline

- Draw a timeline of your healing journey so far. Mark key moments—both setbacks and breakthroughs. What patterns do you see? What moments of growth stand out?

2. Letter to Your Future Self

- Write a letter to yourself one year from today. Describe where you hope to be emotionally, spiritually, and mentally. What lessons from this season do you want to carry forward?

3. Creating a "Healing Plan"

- Healing doesn't happen by accident. Write down 3-5 steps you can take to actively rebuild your life—this might include therapy, journaling, joining a support group, or setting boundaries in relationships.

4. The Mirror Exercise: Seeing Yourself Differently

- Stand in front of a mirror and say three things that you love about yourself today. Then, say three things you are working toward. Speaking affirmations out loud can reinforce personal growth and self-worth.

5. The Strength Jar

- Every day, write down one thing you did that showed resilience, strength, or growth, and put it in a jar. At the end of the month, read them all to remind yourself how far you've come.

Key Terms List

1. **Resilience** – The ability to adapt and rebuild after adversity.
2. **Post-Traumatic Growth** – The process of finding deeper meaning, strength, and wisdom after experiencing trauma.
3. **Faith Reconstruction** – The act of redefining and strengthening one's faith after a crisis.
4. **Self-Compassion** – Extending kindness and understanding to yourself in times of struggle.
5. **Boundaries** – Limits set to protect emotional well-being and personal growth.
6. **Emotional Recovery** – The process of regaining stability and healing after a period of intense distress.
7. **Redemptive Purpose** – The belief that pain and suffering can lead to renewed purpose and clarity.

8. **Transformation Through Trials** – The idea that hardship refines and reshapes us for the better.
9. **Empowerment** – The process of taking control of your healing and future after loss or betrayal.
10. **Personal Rebirth** – The experience of emerging from hardship as a stronger, wiser, and more authentic version of yourself.

Final Thoughts

Life will break you. But it will also rebuild you.

And when you rise from the ashes, you will see—you were never meant to stay in the fire.

The journey from **ashes to beauty** is not about pretending the fire never happened—it's about **choosing to rise from it**.

Healing isn't about erasing pain; it's about **learning to live fully despite it**.

You are rebuilding. You are transforming. And most importantly—you are rising.

Chapter Ten

The Great Awakening

(Ephesians 5:14 - "Wake up, sleeper, rise from the dead, and Christ will shine on you.")

Still Standing: The Aftermath of the Storm

There's a moment after the storm—after the worst of it has passed, after the chaos has settled—when you realize **you're still**

standing. You don't feel whole, not yet, but there's an undeniable truth that hits you: *I survived.*

That's where I found myself in the months after losing my son and watching my marriage crumble. For the longest time, every breath felt like a battle, every morning a weight I wasn't sure I could lift. **Grief had drained me, heartbreak had emptied me, and yet, somehow, I was still here.**

For months, my prayers had been desperate. **I begged.** I begged for peace, for rest, for strength to get through just one more day without feeling like I was drowning. I wasn't asking for joy—not yet. I just wanted to stop feeling like I was being swallowed whole.

And slowly, **piece by piece,** God answered. Not all at once, not in grand gestures, but in small, undeniable ways:

- I asked for sleep, and for the first time in months, I slept through the night.
- I asked for strength, and one day, I realized I could sit in my son's room without falling apart.
- I asked for financial stability, and though I had no idea how I'd make it, **somehow, every bill got paid.**

I used to say, **"God takes care of babies and fools."** And after everything I've been through, I know I've been both. And yet, He carried me through every moment I thought I wouldn't survive.

A Home Reclaimed

One of the biggest signs of my healing was **taking back my space.**

For so long, my home had been filled with **chaos.** Arguments. Doors slamming. Long, painful silences thick with resentment. There was a heaviness in the air, a feeling of suffocation I had lived with for years but never truly acknowledged until I was alone.

But after the storm—after everything—I started seeing my home differently.

I cleaned, not just for order, but for renewal. I opened the windows, let fresh air in, let light pour into places that had been shadowed for too long. I played music, filled the rooms with sound that wasn't tension or grief. I rearranged furniture, painted walls, and reclaimed every inch of my house from the ghosts of what once was.

I could finally walk through my home **without feeling the weight of the past pressing down on me.** I could sit at my kitchen table and drink tea in silence—**but a silence that felt peaceful, not lonely.** I could look at pictures of my son and smile instead of breaking down.

I had spent so long trying to force peace into my life, **not realizing that peace doesn't come in noise or distraction—it comes in stillness.**

And for the first time, my home was truly mine. Not just the building, but the feeling of it. **It was safe. It was sacred. It was whole.**

Better Than Before

The journey isn't linear. **Grief still lingers.** There are days when the pain sneaks up on me in unexpected ways—a song, a smell, a memory so vivid that it steals my breath.

I still cry. I still carry my grief. **But I am so much better than I was.**

- Better than I was in August, when I thought I would never recover.
- Better than I was in October, when I finally told Warren I was done.
- Better than I was in December, when I spent my first holiday season truly alone, but truly at peace.

And I know this: **I am exactly where I am supposed to be.**

I don't have all the answers. I don't understand every piece of God's plan. **But I know I still have so much to live for.**

This isn't the end of my story. **It's the beginning of something new.**

Love Never Dies—It Finds New Places to Grow

Grief has a way of making you feel like everything has been stripped away—like the love you poured into someone has nowhere to go, floating aimlessly, untethered. **It leaves you feeling empty, lost, and desperate for a way to hold on to something that no longer physically exists.**

But love never truly dies. **It shifts. It transforms. It finds new places to grow.**

I see that truth every day in my little cousin, **Nylah.** She's five years old, a burst of energy and joy wrapped up in a tiny frame, and she adores her "Cousin Toni." Her giggles fill the spaces that once felt too quiet. Her hugs remind me that love still exists, that I still have so much to give.

Some of the love I used to pour into my son, I now pour into her. **Not as a replacement, but as a continuation.** My love for my son will never fade, but I have learned that love is too powerful to stay locked away in grief. **It needs to be shared, to be given, to be lived.**

Losing my son didn't take away my passion for children. If anything, it deepened it. It made me even more aware of how precious every moment is, how fleeting time can be. So now, I love louder. I show up more. **I embrace every opportunity to pour into the people in my life.** Because healing doesn't mean forgetting—it means finding ways to live with the loss while still choosing love, still choosing joy.

The Power of Forgiveness

One of the biggest hurdles in my healing wasn't just processing grief. It wasn't just moving forward. **It was forgiveness.**

Not just forgiving Warren for all the ways he failed me. **But forgiving myself.**

I used to ask myself **a thousand 'what ifs.'** What if I had done more? What if I had noticed something sooner? What if I had been home that day instead of on a work trip? Could I have saved him? Could I have changed the outcome?

Those questions haunted me. **But grief is cruel like that—it tricks you into believing that love alone could have changed fate.**

The truth is, I **did** do enough. **I gave my son a good life.** I raised him with love, provided for him, gave him every opportunity I could. I mothered him fiercely, and that realization—though painful—brought me peace. **My job was done, and I did it well.**

But forgiving Warren? That was different.

He had let me down **in moments I needed him most.** He had made choices that hurt me deeply, that added to my pain instead of relieving it. The bitterness I carried toward him felt justified, **but it also felt heavy.**

At some point, I had to make a decision: **Was I going to carry that weight forever?**

Holding onto resentment didn't hurt Warren—it hurt **me.** It kept me tethered to pain, locked in a cycle of replaying everything he had done wrong, every time he had failed me. And the truth was, **I didn't want to be trapped in that anymore.**

God forgives me daily. **Who am I not to extend that same grace?**

Forgiveness didn't mean forgetting. It didn't mean excusing the past or pretending that everything was okay. **It meant releasing the power it had over me.**

It meant choosing my own freedom.

So I let it go. Not for Warren. Not for anyone else. **But for me.**

Because the only way to truly heal is to stop carrying the things that are breaking you. And I finally decided: **I deserved to be free.**

A Life Worth Living

Finding Purpose Beyond the Pain

Grief and loss have a way of stripping life down to its rawest form. **They force you to see what truly matters—what's worth your time, your energy, and your heart.**

For me, that means choosing peace over chaos, choosing healing over resentment, and choosing to take care of myself in ways I never have before. I spent so many years pouring into others, carrying responsibilities that weren't always mine to bear. Now, I'm learning how to pour into myself. **How to stand in the light of my own life without feeling guilty for wanting joy.**

I don't have all the answers yet. **I don't know exactly where this next chapter will lead me.** But I do know one thing—I'm not done. I still have more to give.

I've always been a giver. It's in my nature to nurture, to uplift, to protect. That hasn't changed. **But now, I'm learning how to do it without losing myself in the process.**

Maybe I won't go back into foster care, but that doesn't mean I'm done making an impact. There are programs that need mentors, children who need guidance, communities that need strong voices. **And I have a voice. I have wisdom, experience, and a heart that refuses to stop loving just because it's been broken.**

And more than anything, I have a life to live.

For so long, I was in survival mode. Now, I want to thrive. I want to **travel** to places I've only dreamed of, **taste food that makes me close my eyes and savor the moment,** and surround myself with people who bring laughter and light into my world. **I want to live boldly and freely because after all the storms, I'm still standing.**

And if I'm still here, that means **my story isn't over yet.**

Lessons from the Awakening

If there's one thing I want people to take from my journey, it's this: **Never give up.** No matter how dark it gets, no matter how lost or broken you feel, there is always hope. **Even if you can't see it yet.**

Here's what I know for sure:

1. **Never give up on yourself.**
   Even when the world feels like it's against you, even when it seems like you have nothing left to give—**you are stronger than you think.**
2. **Set boundaries.**
   Be a giver, love deeply, pour into others—but don't

lose yourself in the process. **Your well-being matters just as much as anyone else's.**

3. **Know when to say no.**
   Protect your peace, your energy, and your time. **Not everyone deserves unlimited access to you.**

4. **Believe in second chances—but not for those who refuse to change.**
   Forgiveness is powerful, but it doesn't mean welcoming back those who repeatedly hurt you. **You can let go without letting someone back in.**

5. **Hope is a choice.**
   Some days, hope will feel easy. Other days, it will feel like a battle. **Wake up every day and choose to believe that better days are coming.**

Because they are.

And so am I.

Discussion Questions for the Reader

1. **The Moment of Awakening**

    - Think about a time when you felt like you were waking up from a long period of struggle or pain. What changed in you that made you realize it was time to move forward?

    -

2. **The Power of Forgiveness**
   - Forgiveness isn't always about others—it's also about freeing yourself. Who or what have you had to forgive in order to find peace? How did that act of forgiveness transform you?
3. **Redefining Purpose**
   - After hardship, our definition of success, happiness, and purpose often changes. How has your vision for your life evolved after overcoming your challenges?
4. **Strength in Reflection**
   - If you could have a conversation with the version of yourself who was at their lowest point, what would you say to them?
5. **Leaving a Legacy**
   - When you think about the story of your life, what do you want to be remembered for? What steps can you take today to ensure you're living in alignment with that vision?

Practical Exercises

1. Writing a Letter to Your Past Self

- Write a letter to the version of yourself who was struggling the most. Offer them the wisdom, reassurance, and encouragement that you now have.

2. The Rebirth Vision Board

- Create a vision board that reflects who you are becoming—not just goals, but the emotions, relationships, and experiences you want to cultivate in this next season.

3. Identifying Strength Through Challenges

- Make a list of the most difficult moments in your life. Next to each one, write down the strength or lesson you gained from it. See how even the hardest seasons have contributed to your growth.

4. The Power of Gratitude and Future Thinking

- Every day for one week, write down three things you are grateful for **now** and three things you are excited about in the **future**. This shifts your mindset from survival mode to an empowered, forward-focused perspective.

5. The Future Self Reflection

- Close your eyes and imagine yourself five years from now. Where are you? What have you accomplished? How do you feel? What advice does your future self have for you today? Write down that advice as a guiding reminder.

Key Terms List

1. **Awakening** – The realization that it is time to step into purpose, healing, and strength.
2. **Self-Renewal** – The ongoing process of personal transformation and growth.
3. **Redemptive Healing** – The ability to take past pain and use it as fuel for a greater purpose.
4. **Faith Activation** – Choosing to actively live out one's faith rather than passively believing.
5. **Purpose Alignment** – Ensuring that your daily actions align with your true values and mission.
6. **Empowered Living** – Taking full control of your choices, mindset, and future after overcoming hardships.
7. **Resilience Blueprint** – The lessons, strategies, and mindset shifts that help you navigate future challenges with strength.
8. **Legacy Creation** – The impact you leave on the world through your actions, words, and contributions.

9. **Authentic Joy** – The deep and unshakable sense of peace and fulfillment that comes from living in truth.
10. **New Chapter Mentality** – Understanding that no matter what you've been through, you always have the power to start fresh.

The Final Awakening

I've been writing since the sixth grade. My son, Baby Boy, published his first short story before I did. He saw me writing, saw me working toward something, and he followed in my footsteps. And now, as I close this book, I know this is just the beginning.

I wrote this book to tell my story, but also to remind you of yours. To remind you that you can rise from the ashes, that you can find strength in the wreckage, that you can still create something beautiful even after life breaks you.

So here's my final word:
Wake up.
Rise.
Shine.

Your story isn't over yet either.

Made in the USA
Columbia, SC
30 June 2025

59929870R00107